Ginnie

I0487221

Finds
Her
G-Spot

Desiree

Davidson

Desiree Davidson

Worldwide-Erotica

Ginnie Finds Her G-Spot

DEDICATION

In remembrance of our Hunter,
Friend and Story Teller:

Gary V. Kieffer

We Will Always Remember You.

Desiree Davidson

Desiree Davidson

CONTENTS

Desiree Davidson

Ginnie Finds Her G-Spot

Ginnie had only limited sexual experience at age thirty. She was with two boys before she got married and her husband and one other nice older man after she married. Yes Ginnie was a neophyte but her next door neighbor was working to change that.

Ginnie had told Liz that she could only reach orgasm orally or with a vibrator. Her husband had bought her one to liven up their sex life. Now Ginnie was still only coming with clitoral stimulation but it felt wonderful! She would lie in bed for a long session of coming. She told Liz what she was doing and Liz told Ginnie that she should have another woman's touch for her playtime. Ginnie had a friend in High School that liked to be with other girls. They had never done anything but her friend had given her the details and she knew it was exciting. What would be wrong with inviting Liz into her bed to share her playtime.

Liz was more than ready to be with Ginnie and readily accepted when she invited her.

***

Ginnie was the first to undress fully and stretch out on the bed. Liz took a longer time to undress so Ginnie would appreciate the erotic flavor of the moment. Liz lay down beside her and told her she had brought a special present for her. But first Liz initiated a kissing session and Ginnie seemed particularly interested in fondling Liz's breasts - hers being a firm D compared to Ginnie's C-cup. Her blondness was in sharp contrast to Liz's sleek raven black hair. The contrast alone was as sexy as you could get. They were two beautiful young women.

Liz asked for the vibrator and Ginnie gave her a small one designed for direct clitoral stimulation. Liz applied it expertly and very quickly Ginnie was coming stronger than she had ever came. Liz let her have three sets of orgasms before she suggest that she would like to have Liz do her orally. Liz eagerly bent to the task and had Ginnie going wild on the strength and length of orgasm.

Ginnie wanted to return the favor and was very shortly burying her face in Liz's raven black pussy. Liz came quickly several times and then the two of them lay and touched each other as they enjoyed the afterglow of their sex session.

It was then that Liz said she had brought Ginnie a present. Liz got up and went to her bag and brought back a sex toy. Ginnie was puzzled by the bent up end of the vibrator. Liz quickly explained that it was designed to stimulate her G-Spot.

Ginnie had read magazines in Cosmo and elsewhere but when she or Rick tried to stimulate it with their fingers, it did nothing for her. She told Liz of their tries.

Liz asked to put her fingers in Ginnie's vagina to feel for her G-spot. Ginnie had a large G-spot palpable to the fingers.

Liz told her that she had a prominent G-spot and that she would like to use the "bent" vibrator to jet her off. Ginnie lay back down and Liz inserted the toy and turned it on. In only a few moments, Ginnie body was wracked with strong waves of pleasure and it seemed to her that she would never stop coming. Liz let Ginnie have the vibrator and she watched as her friend had her most exciting sexual experience.

Ginnie had found her G-spot!

When Ginnie came down from her high, She faced Liz and kissed long passionate kisses with Liz. She trembled from the wonderful experience she had and lay in Liz's arms recovering.

Desiree Davidson

Liz held her and prepared her for the next part of their adventure.

This was a first time with Liz, but Ginnie was certain that she was going to be a frequent visitor to her house..

Desiree Davidson

On the Edge

She went to the pool late in the day. There were a handful of kids and their mothers and two young Black men. Her husband was on a trip and to be perfectly honest, she was horney. She had used her vibrator and come several times, but what she really needed was her husband's long thick dick to make her come while he fucked her.

The kids and their mothers thinned out and as the sky grew dusky but before the pool lights came on, she was left alone with the two young men. They were 19 to 22 she thought, but it was hard to judge the age of young Black men. She was 40 but looked 30. Her light green bikini set off her blonde hair and did little to cover her large firm breasts. The bottom showed lots of cheek and she had trimmed her blonde pussy hair so there was not a single strand peeking out from the tiny bikini bottom.

Rachel was floating upright in the deep end of the pool and there was a flotation chair left there so she took it in tow and swam one handed toward the shallow end of the pool. As she passed she bumped into one of the two Black men.

Rachel said, "I'm sorry – I hope that didn't hurt. Jamaal said, "No, Let us get that for you" and took the chair and lifted it out of the pool and left it at the edge.

Rachel had used the chairs to float in the pool a number of times and they were quite comfortable to recline in.

Jamaal went back to Denel and Janet came over to thank them for helping her.

Jamaal and Denel were wearing swim trunks that clung to their bodies. It was somehow gratifying to still look good enough and exude sexiness enough at 40 that both men were showing obvious signs of getting hard – pool shrinkage was obviously not a factor here.

Janet was on the deeper side and took their arms to keep her afloat. At 5'2", 110 pounds and naturally big busted she could float or she could stand, but only if the water was shallow enough. Janet asked their names and told them hers and asked if they lived in the complex. They said they were visiting their friend and he had gone up to take care of some business but should be back soon.

Rachel's cunt was on fire. She hadn't been fucked in four days and couldn't wait till her husband came home.

The sky was growing darker but it would be a while before the pool lights came on.

The men had been eying her big breasts and were both fully hard. She decided that she would have to initiate what she wanted. It was simple enough –

"Would you guys like to fuck me?" Rachel said.

There was silence for a long period and then each one confirmed they would love to give the pretty blond their big Black cocks.

Rachel told them to bring the floating chair back into the pool and both saw what she had in mind when she got into the chair with her legs open and dangling into the water. Denel pulled her bikini bottom from her legs and Jamaal pulled his trunks off and revealed a thick cock about 10inches in length. He moved the chair out into the water to where his hungry Black dick was positioned at Rachel's cunt and Denel kept the chair steady in the water while his friend fucked her pretty White pussy.

Rachel said, "Take your time – be sure and come in me –don't pull out – your dick feels wonderful – I want to feel you come in me."

At the same time, Rachel began coming on his big Black dick and could only cry out in pleasure.

Jamaal came in Rachel flooding her womb with hundreds of millions of Black sperm. When he finished, he stepped aside and steadied the chair while Denel entered Rachel. He was very thick but only about eight inches in length.

Denel entered Rachel very easily thanks to her natural wetness and his friend going first and saturating her cunt with semen. Denel in only a few strokes had Rachel coming again. It was exciting to do something she had never done before --let a Black man fuck her. Rachel scooted down to get every stroke of this young Black stud. Denel was in a hurry and quickly began to dump his big Black balls into Rachel's little blonde cunt. Rachel longed for more fucking. Rachel's wish was granted -- there was another and almost as soon as Denel pulled out of her pussy their friend stepped between her legs and rapidly fucked her to orgasm with his long thick Black dick. Even a third was not enough. She moved off the chair into the water and

streams of cum flowed out of her dilated cunt and floated away into the water.

One of the Black studs gave her the bikini bottom and steadied her while she slipped it back on. He was the last to trunk up and finished just at the pool lights came on.

Rachel pulled each one's face to her and kissed them and told them what wonderful studs they were. Then she had a wicked thought and acted on it. She invited all three to her apartment to fuck them properly -- singularly and in combination.

Rachel was impaled with one Black dick in her cunt and one in her ass when her husband called. She told the one she was sucking off to get the cordless phone for her. She told her new Black friends to be very quite. Then she answered his call and told him she was doing good but missed him and wished she could have his cock right now. They flirted a while and then she quickly hung up because she was coming and crying out in pleasure from being doubled by two delicious Black dicks.

Desiree Davidson

One Summer

I was out shopping for a few hours one day in early summer of '63 and Pamela had the run of the house and I guess it was time for her. I had answered some of her remaining questions the week before. She went down to the drugstore to get a Coke and some air conditioning for it was so very hot all that summer. There you were, a nice guy she knew, and you wanted to know her very well. As she told it to me, you bought her a second coke and after talking for awhile, suggested you walk her home and get to know each other even better. You were 13 and she was 14 and behind a year and had been in school with you in the spring. She invited you in, and the two of you, sitting on the couch, watching nothing on TV, began to pet. She said she started it. She quickly found you knew more than how to kiss and more than how to touch her, or as she said, 'Mama, I had never felt the way Eric was making me feel!' She moved things along, and as you say, you gave her your special invitation, and it was time for her to choose. Looking back, after all these years, we chose well, but there was a time in the fall of that year when we weren't so sure, but our doubts passed the following year. There always has to be a first time for every girl, and she had decided you were definitely hers. She had waited because I had not and she was born when I was 17.

Knowing, she had a couple of hours before I would be home, and having thought carefully about it, she led you down the hall and showed you her room. She went to the bathroom and when she came back you had turned her bed down and you asked her if she was sure she wanted you. She nodded. She told me that standing there you touched her and kissed her, and asked if this was her first time, and receiving a yes, you told her that this would be so gentle, so easy, that she would want to play all afternoon.

You then undressed her and lay her down. It was hot even with the window fan on full, and you cracked the door for a little circulation. She was concerned about the four to five inches of open door, but you reminded her I wouldn't be home for a couple of hours. As you moved to her, she said you were very gently kissing her, fondling her breasts, sucking and touching her nipples, and kissing and stroking her body,

when you suggested making her come with the best kisses of all. We had talked about that being the way most girls reach orgasm, and she wanted to try.

She said after that unforgettable first orgasmic experience, you asked to explore her with your fingers. She told me it was nice and when you were finished, you told her she was very wet and relaxed and although the fit would still be snug, it would be pleasant and if she really wanted too, then she was ready to make love. You went on and told her that her hymen was very thin and small, and even though her first lover was going to be somewhat large, you would like to be hers now.

She said it didn't even hurt, and it felt great as she became a woman when you gently pushed into her. When you began to move, she said she felt like coming and did, just like when you had kissed and tongued her so sweetly at first. She came, when you made love to her for her very first time! She said after a very long time, she felt your strong long pulses as you finished completing her woman hood. Then you gently pulled out of her, moved from her wrapped legs, and lay beside her. You continued to love her with kisses and words and touches, and she said your hardness felt wonderful, it strongly pushed against her body, and she knew it was insisting you wanted her more.

The one thing she asked me about was that experience. She said from the moment she petted with you on the couch and after having come in her several times, you had never lost your hardness. I told her, "Baby, it just doesn't happen that way with men--you must be mistaken!" She was pretty insistent you had remained that way as the two of you continued delighting in each other, throughout the afternoon.

You taught her some fun positions and interesting things to do. The next to last time, you had her positioned 'woman astride.' You both had lost track of time. As I came in the house and passed the head of the hall, mixed in with the fan noise, I heard what I thought was me vocalizing my orgasms! Then I realized the voice was younger–my Baby! I fought myself. Not wanting to interrupt those sounds, and yet at the same time, I had to at least see that Pamela was alright.

I quietly walked down the hall and through the opening of Pamela's door. I could see the two of you making love. 'This is my

Desiree Davidson

Baby's first time?' quickly flashed through my mind. She was coming over and over again as she bounced so very hard up and down on you. I wondered if my daughter had lied to me about being a virgin all the times we had talked about sex, starting when she was 11, and most recently just last week. She certainly didn't look like one, then.

When she finished, your semen dripped out of her as she lay down on your chest. You were pinned beneath her and you had only partially come for you continued, for a considerable time, to seep out between your nestled sides. She'd dismounted too soon, and it was obvious you weren't finished with her yet. As I had this thought, I realized you were looking straight into my eyes and you seemed not to be disturbed I was there watching you. I recalled my previous thought, and I turned and silently walked down the hall and out of the house and let the two of you continue.

My husband wouldn't be home for three hours and I decided to give you two, to continue my daughter's education and for her to reward you by sending you away satisfied. When I came back, you were gone and she was clothed and asleep on her bed. My husband came home and asked where Pamela was. I told him she'd really done too many things today with one of her friends and she was sleeping, and probably was much too tired to wake before morning. The next morning, my husband was off to work, and Pamela came running down the hall to the kitchen calling out that she really needed to talk. Just hearing her recount her first adventure, was almost more than I could stand–not from anger, and not from concern for her, but from vicarious excitement.

She told of a beautiful experience. But I had to remind her we'd talked about the importance of using protection. I reminded her that they were in my nightstand and always available to her without question. Then Pamela told me she obtained them from my room and had tried, but then consciously chose not to use them. She continued to say your bare skin felt so good and she didn't think she could come any other way. For this mother, this wasn't very re-assuring for the future. For, I knew from her description of her first time, you'd be with my daughter any time she wanted you and any time you wanted her. It would be a good while before she tried a second guy as long as you were available. As she had said, 'You were just so much fun! I don't

want another guy, he's my first, he's amazing, and I want him for a very long time. I chose the right one!'

As far as I know, I was the only boy she was with that summer. She wanted to make love all the time and she became almost too much to handle as she wanted to explore everything she'd ever heard about and expected you to keep up with her amazing body, and then she had an imagination for new things to try. She found that, yes, you had the stamina for most of her adventures, but you were certainly not 'endless' in anyway.

One day when you were coming out of the drugstore, I was walking down the sidewalk right toward you, and I had an expression of foreboding.

I walked right up to you and said, "We've got to talk! Will you come with me to my house?"

You said, "Sure Mrs.…"

We walked to my car and drove a few blocks to my house.

It was burning hot and I was dressed for it. My pink shorts, white midriff blouse, light pink jewelry, and sexy pink sun glasses made me feel cool, even if it was not. My long black hair shimmered in the sun. You followed me in. You waited for me to settle things in the kitchen and give some direction to this meeting.

I told you to set down at the kitchen table, and when you were seated, I turned around and leaned over the table and took my sun glasses off and you looked into my grey blue eyes, a perfect match for your beautiful long black hair. I could feel your eyes caressing every part of my body. I was a 'hot' mom! And not because the house was stifling, except I did feel a hint of a cool breeze from down the hall. My husband had installed a window air conditioner in the master bedroom. Pamela hold told me that you'd enjoyed the cool with her on three visits. When she first led you to my room instead of hers, you had balked. She explained I had told her she could use my bed with her friend, and reminded her to be on your side by your night stand so she would have no problem remembering to use protection.

You smiled at me as you continued to look at me and when I smiled back, I knew you wanted to possess me. My look softened, and I became friendly. I offered you some ice tea, and we sat at the kitchen table. It seems like only yesterday.

Desiree Davidson

Eric, I was mad. Although it was OK, what you and Pamela were doing, it wasn't OK that you two were not using protection. Pamela was my gift at age 17 for not having protection when I had my first time at age 16! Pamela, told me you were always willing, but she wasn't, because you couldn't penetrate her fully without pulling off, or breaking, or even failing one just getting it on.

"Do you know how to properly use protection?" I asked.

You replied, "Yes, but that's not exactly the problem."

I then took up my daughter's complaint and asked you if it was really because she thought bare feels so much better.

"Well it does." you said. "But we both want to protect her from pregnancy if we can, but oral is not enough for her anymore–she's way beyond that now, having had me for her first, and she has embraced more diverse adventures with every one of the follow on seven sessions since her first."

I then firmly told you that condoms did protect against pregnancy, but they also protected against disease. You told me you knew, but you had never had anything, but you hadn't had much experience, Pamela was your 199th lover. I admit at that moment, all Pamela had told me and that brief 'my own eyes' experience of seeing the two of you together the first time, flashed through my mind. My God! I thought. You are 13 what will your count be in 20 years? Then I rejected it as fantasy and didn't want to believe it.

I asked, "If you had said 9th partner?"

You calmly said no. Then almost in a reverie you said, "I want my 200th soon, no later than this summer."

I said, "Does anyone know about you?"

At age 13, you told me you never told anything unless it was life critical–all of your life was a secret. You told me you particularly never told anyone about your encounters. You said only you and your partner knew who you were and the details of your private encounters. If your passion was public, it would be like the brags of guys saying they had been with someone when actually they were virgins themselves.

"I never tell anything!" you said.

I changed the subject, for I was 31 years old and sexually active since age 16 and I had been with 18 men other than my husband, and I thought I was somewhat advanced in those very private times of the

50's and early 60's before birth control pills changed thinking, even in the Bible Belt. I was feeling just a little too curious.

Here, was a boy, loving my daughter, and he had more experience than almost all men gain in a lifetime. But I was burning to know and see what you actually would tell, and I asked what age range you had been with. You told me your oldest was 27 but most were older than you because you looked older. You said you loved girls and women of every age, and you felt certain this summer the upper age would change.

I changed the subject again and talked about other things while I decided what to do. I could leave you with my daughter, I could forbid you to see her--no telling what creep she would then be playing with or I could encourage your safety and gentle teaching of my daughter, and talk with you more about condom use. I chose the last, for Pamela really enjoyed you and you seemed to be a really nice guy and a caring lover, and just as she had volunteered, she and I would have wanted no one else to have been her first.

I recalled my first and I thought I wished he had been you... and that was the thought that got me in trouble. I had stopped to drink some iced tea and as I set the glass down, you looked deeply into my eyes and said I was even more beautiful than my daughter. You continued to tell me everyone needed to have a very special mom like me. I could not stop looking at you as your locking eyes seemed to caress me in that special spot in my mind and then reached in and knew. Yes it would be illegal, and it might be morally wrong, but I wanted to know what you knew that would make me feel as good as you were making my recently virginal daughter feel!

You finally let my eyes go and then I realized you had boldly taken my hand in yours and was softly caressing my palm and fingers very sensuously. I was turned on more than I'd ever been in my life! Although I knew I had to get out of this, I just didn't want to. I thought. Why hasn't Pamela returned? Then, I remembered she had gone with a girlfriend to the next town to swim all day and wouldn't be back till 6 when my husband would pick them up and bring them home.

As you caressed my hand, it was 10 in the morning--what could you do with me until 4, I thought? I cleared my head of that very

dangerous but exciting thought. I said nothing, but I gently moved my hand away, as I got up to get more tea for the two of us.

"I could throw you out," I thought, "But I'd already made my decision to let you be with my daughter."

I focused on that and returned to protection. I covered the same ground again and got the same answer that those things were not the problem, but you were. It was so hot that day that our clothing was getting soaked with sweat. I saw a perfect large banana lying on the side counter. I got up to get it and said that we should be sure. I started to sit down and take some condoms out of my purse which was on the table, but then I remembered that we were in a sweat box. I said it was so hot in here we should go to my air conditioned bedroom and show you how to use a condom. I about fainted as I said it, and realized all the meaning it could have. I remember wondering what meaning it held for you.

I asked you to follow me, and we went down the hall to my bedroom. I sat down on the bed by my nightstand and asked you to sit by me. I opened the drawer and took out four condoms, and handed them to you. I reached over you to lay the banana on your other side because you were very close to me. When I was doing it, I glanced into your lap and you were hard, thick and down your jeans leg and at the end, your jeans were soaked. Must be sweat, I thought, couldn't be anything else. I returned to sanity, sort of. Then I suddenly remembered I'd had only one larger lover before, and although interesting, in a curiosity way, once had been more than enough, for he thought his size was all I needed. I was never with him again. Come to think of it, he claimed he couldn't use condoms, and that day I was about to start my period and nothing happened even though I let him finish in me. I think when I looked in on you and Pamela, her first time, I didn't really look at all of you, for I was thinking of Pamela.

I got back to sanity again and I asked you to tear off one of them, then open it properly and then pretend the banana was you and properly roll the sheath on while pinching the top to maintain a small space for the fluid. You did it perfectly.

I said, "Do another one, and you did."

Then I did one to show you what a woman might do wrong. Watch for her nails on opening and rolling it on by hand or mouth I

said--do be particularly careful of nails in maintaining the space at the end with no damage. As I did it, I thought how lazy my husband had become. Although it was he who didn't want any more 'kids,' he expected me to prepare him either with hand or mouth. I guess this was a refresher for tonight or would it be next week as it had been for a month. I felt dampness in my panties and I excused myself to go to the bathroom.

"My period is coming up and I might have been a day or two early," I thought.

When I looked, it wasn't that, although there was a tiny hint of pink. I was starting, but this wetness was the liquid of excitement. I had become so excited I had soaked my panties and my shorts were soaked all the way through, and showing all over the crotch and beginning down the legs. My forbidden thoughts had me so excited and ready, I had lost my logical mind!

My cute new silk dressing gown was hanging on the bathroom door. It was very thin and cool. I didn't do it with premeditation, but I took off all my clothes and put on the cute little, thigh-length buttoned gown. I walked out and there you stood with the bed turned down and facing me. I startled and froze.

You asked, "Did I misunderstand? Did you not accept my invitation?"

I didn't answer. You walked to me and stood looking longingly in my eyes, caressed my face with those wonderful fingers of yours and asked me if I was sure I wanted you.

I whispered, "Yes."

Eric you removed my dressing gown, kissed me and told me how beautiful I was and how kind it was I had decided to be your 200th. You laid me down and kissed me, caressed me, touched me and explored me and all the while told me all the reasons at age 31, I was more beautiful than my daughter. You were magnificent and you spent the next 5 hours showing me that you had learned a great many things in your encounters and practice. I'd had those condoms in my purse for a reason, and after your first time breaking the 30 barrier and my first time being with a young lover, I returned them to the drawer and was never with my other man again. You met every need. Over the summer you continued with Pamela and with me, and I don't believe there

could have ever been a more satisfied mother and daughter. With first hand experience, I did learn why the problem was you. Apparently, through the years, all of your lovers have chosen their own way.'

"Eric, when we moved at the end of summer, you told Pamela and me, you would remember us always, and you were sure you would see us again. You never forgot us and we never forgot you. We moved away at the end of that summer, and the next year, both of us had your babies. Two boys! Now both are 43 and they have a lot of children. You head huge families with both girls and boys. They are, so beautiful! You make good descendants!

Desiree Davidson

Sex by the Lines

Fall came and I decided to approach an attractive older woman again. I knew Mrs. 'W' (Janet) from her participation in my school plays. She assisted our English teacher with the sets and technical set up. Janet had a daughter my age, but I really didn't know her very well.

Our English teacher was sick around the time we were supposed to be running lines for the upcoming play and my opposite actress was sick that week as well; so Janet ran lines with me. She was funny, personable, bright, and cute. She told me she was 35 years old and I was going to find some way to seduce her.

Janet had green eyes and long brown hair. She was cute; her personality just made me want her more. She had a perfect C-cup and great legs. She tended to wear short skirts, and when she was working on a ladder placing a set, I caught a quick glimpse of her long shapely legs.

I found my opening. I faked having trouble memorizing my lines and asked if she could help me after school. She agreed. It was the perfect day. School was out early for some maintenance work, her daughter Jean Ann was in the band and they had gone on an overnight band competition. Her husband was a salesman and he was on the road for the week. We couldn't run lines at school because of the electrical maintenance, so Janet took me home with her.

Circumstances could not have brought me a better opportunity if I had the power to control all these events.

We sat at her kitchen table for a while and had some hot tea to drink and then after about an hour of running lines at the table, we moved to the sofa in the family room. She sat down first and I sat down as close to her as possible without spooking her. I was very mature for my age, looked older and I was taller than Janet. I was determined to seduce this lovely woman.

Janet had on a tight v-neck sweater top and its turquoise color was a striking contrast to her cream colored linen skirt. She was wearing heels that matched her sweater and she was a living doll.

We were running lines for my part, and I noticed she put a pillow behind her back and grimaced.

I said, "Janet I want to make love to you!"

There was a long awkward pause; then she stood up and took off the robe as I pulled off my boxers. We returned to the bed and I began kissing her and fondling her breasts as she stroked my cock and realized I was significantly bigger than her husband. She reached in the night stand and brought out a condom package and tore it open and tried to put it on my big cock. It was hopeless, the first broke as she attempted to roll it on and the second only covered about 6 inches of my thick cock before it broke too.

Janet said, "Forget the condoms; I really want you to cum in me anyhow."

I moved between her legs and found she was not ready for me, so I lay between her legs and gave her the best kiss of all as I tongued her clit until she came several times. The stimulation caused her to grow wet and relaxed and she took my cock and guided it into her.

"God! You're big," she said.

"You have just the perfect slit to handle it," I replied.

Her pussy felt great when I was fully in her. I allowed her to adjust to my thickness and length and then I began to fuck her. We fucked for more than ten minutes and at about the five minute mark Janet began to come on my cock and kept it up until I exploded and filled her pussy with my cum.

I moved out of her still hard and I fondled her breasts and kissed her in the afterglow of the moment.

"She said, "When you came in me you pulsed over and over again, I must be full of your come."

"I'll take care of that," I said

I doubled a pillow under my head and asked her to straddle my face so I could eat my warm cum out of her pussy and bring her to one marvelous orgasm after another. After awhile she moved down my body and impaled her firm body on my cock and took me in the woman astride position. She rode furiously and I felt her strong orgasms squeeze my cock over and over. She brought me to the brink of coming several times and then finally I shot streams of cum into her body again.

She said, "Eric that was wonderful, I've never come like that!"

Desiree Davidson

She moved beside me and laid her head on my hairy chest. I traced her pretty full lips with my finger tip and told her how beautiful she was.

I asked' "How is your back now?"

She said, "With all those orgasms, I don't feel a thing. I'll take you as my pain reliever regularly."

Janet moved up and kissed me with long passionate kisses. I knew it was getting late and although she had a fully open schedule, I did not. I asked her what time it was and she looked at the clock radio and told me it was just after 5 pm. I had to go then. In the next few days, we found ways to be in each others arms three times.

Later in November, I was with her another seven times and every time was better than the last as we learned to better pleasure each other.

Desiree Davidson

Raining

I was on a business trip and decided to go down in the Italian neighborhood of Cleveland, Ohio and find an authentic Italian restaurant. I drove down the narrow streets and saw one I'd like to try but all the street parking was full and I had to park eight blocks away and walk back. When I walked in there was an attractive woman asking to be seated at a table for one.

In those moments she stood talking to the hostess I decide I wanted her.

It was late fall and the weather was variable. She had on a green knit sheath dress that hugged her curves. On close examination it was obvious that there were no bra or panty lines visible. That intrigued me.

She had somewhat of a square face but she was quite attractive in her own unique way. Her hair was medium wheat colored blond and due to the varying shades of the primary color it was highly likely that she was a natural.

She wore spike heel boots and she was without hose. The ivory color of her face was repeated in her bare legs.

She was by anyone's measure a woman to be pursued.

The hostess took her away and seated her in the back of the restaurant and then returned to greet me. I told her I needed a table for one, but could she seat me near the beautiful woman she seated before?

She smiled and said "I will be happy too; this was a place for lovers."

She placed me one table over and seated me in a position so I was facing Toni as I would soon find her name by introducing myself and she in return giving me hers. She was open to conversation and I asked if I could join her at her table and she agreed.

The waiter came and we were occupied for a few minutes, but after he left we began to get to know each other. She was on a business trip too and had to park a number of blocks away just as I had done. The sun was setting and by the time we would be through it would be dark. I asked her if I could walk her to her car after our meal and she said that would be nice.

Desiree Davidson

All during the meal we got to know each other better and as we were having dessert and coffee, I reached over and took her hand. Just touching her was electrifying. I decided to make my move as we walked to her car, but her show of interest in me led me to believe that making love to her was in my future.

I paid the check and we went out of the restaurant. In the night sky there were threatening storm clouds and lightning.

We held hands as we walked and suddenly the sky let loose with a torrential downpour. We were about four blocks from the restaurant and getting soaking wet. There was a small covered loading dock that opened on the street and we sought shelter there.

Toni leaned against the brick wall catching her breath and then she said come here. I did not have far to go to be in front of her. Toni took my face and pulled me down to kiss her. After the initial kiss it was totally blurred about who was initiating the next kiss, but there was no doubt about what followed. Toni said, "I want you to fuck me right here in the rain."

I reached for the hem of her sweater dress and pulled it up above her large firm breasts. She had huge nipples and absolutely perfect breasts. I started to bend to them with my mouth but Toni stopped me when she said, "I want you to fuck me now, there will be time for that later."

I moved slightly back and dropped my slacks and shorts and she lifted a leg around my hip and my throbbing cock entered her delicious pussy. I fucked her for only a few minutes and she began to come and kept coming until about ten minutes of fucking, when I shot stream after stream of come into her body. When her last orgasms subsided, I pulled out of her still almost fully erect.

Toni took my hard cock in her hand and she said, "I have to have more of this guy – he's wonderful and so big. Come with me to my hotel where we can continue this more comfortably."

As it turned out, her hotel just happened to be my hotel so loving her was easy.

When we got in her room, we stripped our wet clothes off and got into a hot shower together and got to know each other's bodies more completely.

While we dried each other, Toni said, "Eric, I've never done anything like that, but in the movies it looks so sexually charged that I just had to try it"

"I'm glad you did," Eric replied, "Were you satisfied with your experience?"

Toni said, Satisfied for then, but now I need you to lay me down in that big, soft, king size bed and see how many times you can fuck me before morning."

Desiree Davidson

Sometimes Love's
Not Enough

Our plane was an L1011 with a center section of five seats and two seats on each side of the plane. I was seated in the center section in the right-most seat, and this center section faced the bulkhead. Only one other seat was occupied in my center row so far--a young black man was sitting in the left-most seat. There were three seats between us and I was hoping to raise the arms and stretch out in the four seats and sleep the flight away.

Down the aisle came an attractive young lady dressed in a soft green jogging suit. Her long brown hair cascaded on to the shoulders of her suit. Her seat assignment was next to mine and I stood up and helped her get her large carry-on-bag into the overhead bin. Then I sat down and found her beside me.

"Hi, I'm Eric," I said.

She replied, "I'm Danni."

The flight attendant came on making announcements; she had a California accent which I liked; it was good to be going home. It was hard though to leave my wife and two young boys in Oklahoma for a week after Christmas.

The announcements were over and everyone was buckled up and shortly we were in the air.

"Danni are you going home?" I asked.

"Yes," she said, "I visited my parents in Dallas for Christmas." She asked if I was going home.

"Yes," I replied, "My wife and boys are coming home next week so I'll be at loose ends for awhile."

Danni told me she lived in Ontario.

"I flew out of the airport there since I couldn't get flights out of LA. My car is waiting for me there," I told her.

Danni and I talked during the flight.

She said, "I'm 23 and I'm getting married on Valentine's Day.

Desiree Davidson

I said, "Your wedding day will be the day after my birthday, I will be 32."

Near the end of the flight Danni said, "My fiancée is going to meet me at the airport, you'll have to let me introduce you."

Danni was attractive, bright, amusing, and quick witted--in short she was very likeable. We got along very well and our visiting made the flight pass in a moment. We arrived about midnight and I carried her carry-on-bag to the checked baggage carousel to collect her other three bags and my one.

Danni was ready to leave but there was no fiancée! She called his apartment several times and there was no answer. So I waited with her, for the airport was almost deserted, since we were the last arrival for the evening, and I didn't like the looks of some of the last few people who remained. I told her I didn't think David was coming.

After about 30 minutes, I said, "Let me take you home."

Her apartment was only about 25 minutes out of my way and no one was waiting for me.

Danni agreed.

"I said. I'll get a cart for your three big bags, your carry-on and my one bag and briefcase."

We went to my car and filled up the trunk and back seat with bags. I opened the passenger door and seated her, and then I got in the car and drove away. She gave me very clear instructions on how to get from the airport to her apartment and we got there in about 20 minutes instead of the 25 minutes I had estimated.

Danni was a small young woman and she had packed too much, so I helped her get her bags into her apartment.

After getting the bags in, Danni said, "Why don't you stay for some hot chocolate?"

I said, "I'd love to."

Danni said, "Please sit down in the living room on my new love seat."

She made the hot chocolate and then joined me on the love seat. We talked as we sipped our hot chocolate and we got to know each other better. Danni filled my cup up again and that added an extra half hour to my four hour stay with Danni on the airplane, the airport, the drive and now in her apartment.

Desiree Davidson

I said, "Did you buy your wedding dress while in Dallas?"

She replied, "I bought my entire trousseau."

That explained the heavy bags.

She said, "Let me show you my wedding dress."

She took me to her bedroom to help her with the bags. She got the dress out and also laid out her wedding night gown ensemble. She had me turn my back while she took her jogging suit off and put on the bridal dress. She was still zipping it up when she asked me to turn around and help her zip it all the way up. It was a strapless design and was quite beautiful on her. Her bare back and the skin of her breasts exposed by the low cut front were very attractive. I told her that it was lovely and she was beautiful in it.

After she modeled it for awhile, I unzipped her when she was ready and she took it off, and this time I did not turn around! When she laid the dress on the bed she turned around and had only her panties on. Her breasts were beautiful firm C-cups and she had medium size brown nipples with large brown areolas. Danni was not shocked and did not try to hide anything.

She said, "I hoped you would look. Let me hang this dress up and I'm going to reward you for taking such good care of me on my trip."

I took off my clothes and was naked when she turned around from hanging the dress up. "My God! You're big!" she said, as she took off her panties.

I went to her and took her in my arms and kissed her as I felt her small hand begin to stroke my cock.

"Danni" I said, "I think you should have a memory of this you can have when your David is with you on your wedding night."

She looked puzzled at first, but when I picked up the sheer white outfit and separated the negligee from the gown and laid the gown on the suit cases she began to see. I took the sheer negligee and dressed her in it. I turned down the bed and when she was ready I picked up the 'Bride' and carried her to her bed. I placed her on the bed so the negligee was under her and I opened it and spread it out on each side of her. I had made her a pseudo marriage bed of it.

"You remember this," I said, "when David is your partner!"

Then I moved between her legs and leaned over her and kissed her warm, full lips and spent some time with her delightful breasts--so

young and firm. I took her nipples into my mouth and brought them fully erect with my tongue. Shortly she was relaxed enough and wet enough to take me. Danni took my cock in her hand and guided me into her. Her cunt was fantastic, for it was just the right tightness on my big cock not to be uncomfortable for her and it was very stimulating for me. I slowly made love to her and in a few minutes I was giving her long hard thrusts.

Danni began to come on my cock, and was a little tigress in her cries and actions as I continued to fuck her. After about twenty minutes, I began to come in the pretty 'Bride'. I quite literally emptied my balls into her. The naughty little bitch deserved every stream of cum that she got. Danni was marvelous.

I pulled out of her still mostly erect and she went down on me and made me come again.

Danni asked, "Please spend the night with me."

I didn't need to be anyplace, so I spent the night with her. It was more than memorable, for she took me several ways, before we fell asleep. Then in the morning light, we started fucking all over again.

Desiree Davidson

Hungry for Love

"Can you read my mind?" I thought, as I sat down on a couch in the hotel lobby. Only a table separated us and we were both doing the same thing--looking at the Philadelphia visitors' guide.

She was truly a beautiful woman. She had deep auburn hair framing her classically beautiful face. Even as far away as I was, I could look over my book and catch glimpses of bright emerald eyes. She had just the right number of freckles on her legs and I would love to apply an angel kiss to each one. She wore a dark green silk dress that would hit just above the knee if she were standing; as it was it gave a generous view of her beautiful legs. I was most intrigued by the dress for it had buttons all the way down the front. I have always loved real buttons down the front--they invite me to explore. Her lovely neck was accented by a three strand gold necklace. I know real gold when I see it.

I found a place to eat in the restaurant guide section and I put my book down.

Then I said, "Hi, have you found a good place to eat nearby."

She looked up and smiled and said, "I just found one."

Coincidentally it was the Italian place about six blocks away that I had found.

I said, "I'm Eric, what's your Name?"

She said, "Caroline."

Caroline, "You have a beautiful name--one I had considered for my daughter but my wife and I never had a daughter--just three sons."

I told her I was an engineer and I had come to Philly for a seminar. In fact it was at 10 Penn Center just across the street from our hotel.

Caroline said, "I'm an Abram's Drug Company rep and I am also in town for a seminar. I travel a lot but call Cleveland, Ohio home."

"Caroline," I said, "Let me take you to dinner at 'Soto Ravalli.' We can walk, its only 7 blocks away. It's supposed to be a lovely evening; or we can take a cab."

"Let's walk," she said, "We can see the old city hall that way, and a few other sights."

We got up and left the hotel lobby. The evening air was wonderful for July--it was cool. It was early evening and in about three blocks we did pass Old City Hall. We had walked that distance not holding hands, but now I reached for her hand and Caroline reached for mine and we continued our walk to the restaurant hand-in-hand like two young people.

 "Caroline, I said I'm 51"

"I'm 41 she said."

We made it to the restaurant and were in luck, for immediate seating was available for couples. There was a significant wait for larger parties.

Caroline and I were shown to a cozy table in a more dimly lit corner of the restaurant. The waiter asked if we wanted to order a bottle of wine before dinner. Caroline declined. Since I never drink, this girl was my kind of lady. We ordered and then had a wonderful meal of veal parmesan and followed it with strawberry gelato and espresso. The waiter came and I paid the check. The gelato was gone and dishes taken away and we continued to talk.

Caroline had her left hand lying on the table and I reached across with my left and took it in mine. Caroline's right hand was bare of rings which mine was not--I wear a simple gold wedding band, but on her left was a rather exotic ring of several emeralds exactly the color of her eyes. I asked about it. She said it was given to her by a girlfriend.

"What about your gold ring with the heart and shield on it?" she asked."

I said, "It indicates membership in an age old, secret society. I went on and said that its US temple is here in Philly and I was there last evening, and as a Temple Knight Grand Master Hunter, I was asked to preside over the service with a Grand Master Hunter and a Grand Mistress Huntress of the current course, so all three thrones were filled with me in the middle; 'The Master's Throne.'"

Caroline was interested in the words 'hunter' and 'huntress' and asked about the meaning of the words. And I gave her a brief definition of each.

 "What do you do?" she said.

I replied, "I hunt little girls like you and make passionate love to them."

"Like me, or me," she flirtatiously said.

I said, "It could be others or it could be you; it all depends on your decision."

I held both of her hands across the table and for several minutes we stayed that way. I told her she was a doll for coming to dinner with me because I hated to eat alone--much less not have any beautiful hands to hold. She thanked me for the compliment and for the dinner.

As we walked from the restaurant, I felt her hand searching for mine, and holding hands we set out on our seven block walk back to our hotel. At city hall we stopped for a minute and I pulled Caroline to me and I kissed her and she kissed back. We continued kissing from 'friendly' to 'passionate' in the next five or six minutes and then we continued our walk.

I told her how beautiful she was and how much fun I'd had with her this evening.

We arrived at the hotel and entered the elevator and she pushed her floor button which was three floors below mine.

When I pushed the elevator button for my floor, Caroline said, "Oh, get off with me--I have a suite and we can talk some more and besides I want to give you my card for when you're in Cleveland."

I followed her to her suite and she got us some cold drinks from the mini bar. We sat and talked. I told her about my grown boys--now men and I told her about my beautiful wife who had to do without me because I was always someplace in the world other than Tulsa, Oklahoma, where we had settled after moving most of our married life.

Do you get lonely 'being on the road' so much?" she said.

"I'm always lonely and longing to be with someone," I said.

"It was wonderful of you to go to dinner with me," I said.

Caroline said, "It is lonely for me too. I have had some very bad relationships with men and I've switched camps almost."

I'd heard this story before.

"I still like the right man, but they are so few and far between. You, I like!" she said.

We were setting side by side on the sofa and I leaned over and gently raised her head in my hand and looking directly into her beautiful green eyes I asked her what she liked about me.

Caroline replied, "I like that you make no demands--you expect me to be totally in control of my fate, and you in yours."

I kissed her gently and said, "Well said."

Then I rose to go.

"No, don't go," she said, "Please stay! I have made my decision. Please let's relieve some of our loneliness and longing--stay with me."

I sat back down. She was almost a little girl the way she asked, but she was a beautiful grown woman.

"Do you want to make love with me?" I asked.

"Yes, I want you--I have decided," she said.

"I want you too," I said. "I wanted you from the moment I sat down across from you in the lobby. I want you now!"

With that I stood up and stood her to her feet, and then I took her in my arms and kissed her. Then I picked her up and carried her to the king size bed in the next room. I lay her down on the bed and took her cute high heels from her feet. She had no stockings--that was why I had observed her beautiful freckles. I removed my shoes and then lay down beside her. We lay on our sides and talked some more and I cautioned her that I might be another 'bad experience with a man'.

She said, "You will not be, I know it from all you've said tonight. I am sure I want you and I will never have any regrets."

I reached for her and kissed her passionately, and said, "I will not have any regrets either."

I told her of my button fetish and asked if I could un-button her dress. We moved off the bed and standing face to face I very slowly un-buttoned each one of her buttons. She had a sheer tan colored B-cup bra and matching bikini panties. She did not wear a slip. I removed the dress from her arms and carefully laid it on the chair. Then I removed her bra exposing fully her pert breasts crowned with medium sized reddish brown nipples and small brown areolas. I traced freckles from her breasts down across her belly with my kisses to the band of her bikini panties. I then knelt and slowly lowered her panties to the floor and took them from her feet as she stepped out. I started at her ankles and kissed a trail of freckles up one leg to her pretty auburn mound. I stood up and pulled her to me again and kissed her and told her how beautiful she was. I removed my clothes and the two of us stood naked.

I took her in my arms and picked her up and returned her to the bed. I was hungering badly for her, but I wanted her to be sure.

"Eric your cock looks marvelous!" Caroline said.

I moved between her legs and found her wet and relaxed.

Caroline took my cock in her hand and guided me as I entered her for the first of several times that night. She was marvelous. The tightness of her pussy combined with her silky wetness had me super excited.

I continued long hard thrusts and shortly Caroline began to come.

Oh! God, I'm coming! Don't stop fucking me!" she cried.

I continued long hard thrusts and pushed her to the peak of joy and then I joined her as I shot stream after stream of come into her pretty little cunt.

"You know how to give a man passion in every respect." I said as I collapsed beside her.

In about 15 minutes we were ready again and when you began to come I thrust my big cock deeply into you and filled you again with my come. I stayed hard and began long thrusts again. In another five minutes, I joined your orgasms and erupted in your pussy filling you with stream after stream of creamy white cum.

When we were finished, I went to the bathroom and got a warm wash cloth to clean your delicate cunt. Then I cared for myself and when we were settled again, I lay behind her and kissed freckles for several minutes.

Then both you and I were ready again to make love. Every time was wonderful and our loneliness and longing did abate for a time. We were good for each other.

* * *

My flight had been cancelled and I had to take another flight from Tulsa to Cleveland, Ohio. I was tired but mostly hungry when I checked into my hotel.

When I got to my room I took a quick shower and thought about getting in bed, but I was hungry for food and hungry for sex. I put on a Polo shirt and Dockers and slipped into my loafers. There was a restaurant next door. I would walk over and get something to eat; then

if an opportunity for female company didn't mature, I would come back and get in bed for a few hours rest.

The hostess showed me to a booth and when I got settled, I looked over to the booth across the aisle and it was Caroline the Drug Rep I met in Philadelphia and also a beautiful blonde.

I waved and said, "Hello, Caroline."

She looked up from her drink and said, "Eric! What are you doing in town?"

I said, "The usual--a control systems project--working with a vendor;
Introduce me to your friend."

Caroline said, "Eric this is Carol--we've started living together-- and Carol this is the Eric from Philadelphia."

I went over and said hello to Carol and I bent over and kissed Caroline. Caroline's auburn hair flowed over the shoulders of a long brown ribbed sweater. She was wearing dark jeans and she had on the sexiest high heels. They were brown plaid with a brown ribbon lacing the sides and heel and coming together in the front in a bow above a rounded toe. Carol had on a dark blue jogging suit and sneakers. Her blonde hair was in long curls and fell onto the blue of the suit.

Carol invited me to set down by her, and she scooted over to make room for me. Carol was a blonde delight. I could just feel sexiness radiating from her and Caroline as well. My waiter came with my drink and I told him I would be joining the girls, to bring my food over here.

Carol said, "Did everything Caroline told me happened in 'Philly' really happen?"

I said, "I guess that all depends on what she told you!"

Carol went on in a teasing fashion and said, "Caroline says you're hung like a stallion. Are you?"

My cock was snaked down my left pants leg and was as hard as rock from just looking at these two beautiful women. I took Carol's right hand and placed it in my lap.

"You tell me," I said.

She touched me and began to laugh, and said "He is--he really is!"

I said, "I would be happy to demonstrate it with you two beautiful women." Carol and Caroline looked at each other and then both

nodded. I asked if they wanted to go to my hotel just next door. We finished our food and that's where we went.

I had a suite just perfect for play time, there was king size bed, a couch and two overstuffed chairs and a Jacuzzi tub that actually was open to the bedroom.

As soon as we walked in the door, the girls began to shed their clothes and I followed their lead. In a matter of a minute or two we were three nude sybarites ready to play. I ran the Jacuzzi tub and set the jets, and when I turned around the two little bitches were in a 69 eating each other's pussies. I then realized the full meaning of what Caroline had said in Philly about her ring, because Carol was wearing an identical emerald ring on her left hand. They were bonded bisexuals.

The tub was ready and I got in and relaxed as I watched my little playmates coming and coming with each other. My cock was so stiff from their antics it stood up out of the water.

Carol and Caroline finished with each other with earth shaking orgasms and then joined me in the tub. They were beautiful in the tub with the bubbling water covering their breasts at times and then exposing them. The two were a perfect pair. Both girls had beautiful firm B-Cup breasts and both came with large nipples. Caroline's were brown and Carol's were pink in keeping with her blondeness.

Caroline had soft auburn hair. She scooted over next to me and laid her head on my black hairy chest and sweetly said, "Carol wants you to take her first--make it hard and fast; then it's my turn."

I got out of the tub and helped Carol out. As I dried her off with a big fluffy towel. I spent particular time on her pussy lips and golden haired mound of Venus. Both girls had their hair neatly trimmed. Carol then dried me and spent a special amount of time drying my cock and balls. I thought I was hard before, but now I was really hard and ready for this attractive little girl. When she finished, I picked her up and carried her to my bed. I placed her on it and joined her and moved between her legs. Carol took my cock and placed it in her ready wet pussy and I pushed in slowly.

Caroline, called out, "Remember Eric, fuck her hard and fast--she needs it."

I did just that and very shortly my pretty blond baby was straining all over as wave after wave of orgasms rocked her body. Her tight little

cunt was my cock's end, I began to cum in her pussy and I didn't think I'd ever stop coming in her. Soon both of us were finished and I moved beside her and shared the afterglow of wonderful orgasms.

Carol said, "I want you to lick my clit and make me come again."

I folded a pillow for my head and I had her straddle my face and I began my joyful task. As I stimulated her with my tongue, my two hands were busy fondling her firm little breasts and big nipples.

In a few minutes Carol said, "God, you're good--cock and tongue! I've never come so much with a man. I can't make up my mind which is best your cock or your tongue. I want to ride that cock of yours and see!"

I lay on my back and Carol mounted me in the woman astride position and rammed down on my cock; then she began a wild ride that had her coming and crying at the same time. Suddenly I shot streams of cum into her little body as she had her strongest orgasm. It was so strong that she collapsed on my chest with my cock still in her. She lay there and I picked her face up and gave her a passionate kiss and said we were neglecting Caroline.

Carol and I got back in the Jacuzzi with Caroline and we positioned on each side of her and started intense petting, with Carol and me alternating with deep passionate kisses on her mouth. When she was ready, Carol dried Caroline and herself as I also dried off.

The three of us got on the bed and I was completely hard again. Caroline decided to ride me as Carol had done and Carol wanted to straddle my face again and get her pussy eaten out. A threesome ensued. Caroline felt just as good to my cock as she had in Philly and my little friend, Carol was coming the minute my tongue stroked her clit. The two lovely women were a festival of delights. As I shot my cum into Caroline, Carol was drenching my face in wetness.

The two little sexy bitches finally wore me out and they went back to a 69 girl on girl position and gave me a few minutes to recover and then they were ready to go again. Caroline and Carol spent the night with me and I took them separately and together. When we settled down to sleep I had two 'babes' one on each side lying on my black hairy chest. In the night one or the other would wake me playing with my cock when they were ready to make love again and they mounted me to take a wild orgasmic ride.

Anniversary

His wife Anne had been a virgin when Dan married her. Dan on the other hand had more sex experience packed into his 22 year old life than could be believed. And he marries a woman who values fidelity almost above all other things. Dan was faithful and Anne was faithful for all their marriage, but Dan missed the old variety. Their 36th wedding anniversary was coming up and he always got to ask Anne for a present. Anne was beautiful an ageless woman of 58 years who looked to be in her early 40's.

By any man's judgment Anne was a sexy beautiful woman.

Dan asked for his gift choice and he was dumbfounded when she said yes.

Dan's fingers trembled as he wrote the ad soliciting a man for his wife – you see he'd always wanted to watch. Anne had placed no restrictions other than what she was willing to do to give Dan his anniversary present.

Dan returned to writing his advertisement. This was probably the only chance he'd get, so he might as well raise the stakes. "A young muscular man, well hung and willing to make love to Anne while he watched and joined in." were the words that flowed from his fingers. He knew this was far beyond what Anne had agreed to, but he had a feeling. He attached a seductive picture of Anne with the ad and closed down the computer. About three hours later he began to have second thoughts and decided to go to the computer and cancel his ad and replace it with the one Anne had agreed to. Much to his surprise there were already 37 replies from men wanted his wife. He was amazed and decided to leave his ad alone.

He began to go though the replies and classify them as reject, maybes and definitely.

This process continued the next evening while Anne was out with a friend. He had to work fast for he had 739 replies. He thought he had enough so he was about to stop the ad when one last reply came through – he was a definite but Anne would never be with him in a million years. Dan would love to see it happen though.

The next day at work he spent his lunch hour going through the definite group and looking for the very best one – it still came down to the last man replying. "What would Anne do with him?" Dan thought. Probably not even what she had agreed to and certainly not what Dan would like to see her do with Ted.

The next day Dan called Ted and found they worked in the same building but for different firms. Neither had commitments so they met for lunch at a secluded restaurant where they could have a private conversation.

Dan was up front about the vast difference in sex acts Anne had agreed to and those in Dan's ad and Ted was made aware of one other potential problem. Ted agreed to the limited act and to what Dan really wanted because as he told Dan he could almost feel her riding his dick from just looking at her picture.

After Lunch they went in the men's room which conveniently had low privacy shields between urinals and Ted could quickly prove he as hung as was stated in his ad reply. Dan and Ted sat at the bar a minute and went over the details for next Sunday at the Four Seasons Hotel where the anniversary present was to be given. Dan would reserve two adjoining rooms so he and Ann could be getting ready for this meeting, while Ted undress in the next room and just walk in when he heard the code word.

Sunday came and Ann and Dan went to the hotel room about 6 pm. Dan had rented the rooms and prepared the connecting rooms and left a card key at the front desk for Ted to pick up.

The rules were simple, Anne had agreed to wear a bikini bottom which tied at the side (Dan had insisted on the design and leave her breasts exposed so the man Dan had selected could fondle them if he wanted. The other part of the anniversary gift would be that the man would be fully naked. All Dan told Anne was that the man's name was Ted and he was a muscular young man about 30 years younger than Dan and Ann and that he was the man Dan wanted her to be with. She with some reservation had agreed to satisfy a many years old desire of Dan that he get to watch her suck another man's cock and let him come in her mouth.

Desiree Davidson

Dan undressed completely and watched Anne change out of street clothes and put on the red bikini bottom. Dan hoped it would be coming off too.

Anne turned the king size bed down and lay down. Dan joined her and they spent a long time kissing and fondling as if they were going to make love. Both Anne and Dan were anxious about the coming event but the anxiety seemed to change to sexual excitement for both of them.

Dan maneuvered Anne to the middle of the big bed so he could be on one side and Ted could be on the other.

Dan used a sentence with the code word in it and Ted stepped into the room.

Anne said, "OH my God!"

Dan for a second, thought that Anne's exclamation was because Ted was black, but she continued and said, "Look how big he is!"

Ted was mostly flaccid when he'd walked in the room but seeing Anne's beautiful naked breasts and he mostly naked body, Ted went instantly hard as he walked to the bed where Anne was waiting for him. Ted lay down on the bed and turned on his side toward Anne who understood what he wanted. Anne moved down in the bed so her face was at his cock. He was long and thick – three of her finger wide and by her hands size on it at least twelve inches long. This was not unusual to Anne, her husband who was videotaping this anniversary gift was hung himself but somehow on this muscular black man his black cock seemed even bigger.

Anne stroked him and the head of his cock swelled in anticipation and his huge balls moved in anticipation as well.

Dan was super excited watching his pretty ivory skinned wife examining this black stud he'd found for her. He was ok with Anne's rules, but he wished for more. Regardless he continued to videotape this special anniversary so he could relish it in the years to come – he really thought Anne would cooperate only this once.

Anne began to lick the dark plum colored head of Ted's cock and she found it excited her more than she had ever felt with Dan. As she licked she cradled Ted's ball. Just one filled her hand. "He definitely was a sex machine," she thought.

Ted thought Anne couldn't possibly be 59 as Dan had said. He had been with many women and Anne looked to be 40 to 45. He was

extremely excited and which he could take this beautiful white woman completely – but he was willing to follow Anne's rules.

While Ted was reflecting, Anne had taken the head of his cock in her mouth and more excitement was building if that was possible.

Dan videotaped in close up when Anne had taken the black cock in her mouth. He pushed her blond hair back to get a clear shot as her red lipstick smeared lip prints on the black Shaft.

Time seemed to be standing still but in reality Anne had been sucking Ted for more than ten minutes. Ted had previously curved his back so he could fondle her beautiful breasts and large pink nipples. Now he straightened his back, his balls tightened and his hot cum erupted in Anne's mouth. She couldn't swallow it all - there was just too much – and much spilled out on the sheets. She did purposely keep a mouth full though, as Ted finished with her.

Anne motioned for Dan and he came to her and she French kissed him filling his mouth with Ted's hot cup. She had wondered what he would do and was very surprised that the experience caused her husband to shoot his come all over her abdomen as she gave a few strokes to his erect cock.

Dan went back to videotaping because somehow he thought there3 was more to come.

Anne lay down by Ted and as he touched her breasts She led him into soft kisses and then more passionate. Anne was making up her mind about two things 1) would she let a man other than her husband 2) would she let this handsome black man fuck her! She made her decision.

"Dan, come here and take my bikini bottom off."

It was a command that the two men quickly understood. As Dan untied the sides and pulled the bikini bottom away from his beautiful wife's body, he realized Anne was going to give him what he really wanted.

Ann lay on her back with her legs open and asked Dan to insert his fingers in her pussy to be sure she was ready to take this black stud he'd brought her. He complied and found her wet and ready to give herself to Ted. Ted moved between her legs he was fully recovered

from the oral sex and was ready to fuck her. She took his huge cock and placed the head of his cock into the swollen lips of her pussy.

Dan was busily videotaping again and his 58 year old cock was far from growing hard again.

Ted slowly inserted his cock into her and Anne was on the verge of coming from just letting this black man fuck her. Suddenly she lifted her long legs and encircled the stud's back and fully impaled her cunt on his cock.

She was vaginally orgasmic and almost always came with her husband thrusting in her for ten minutes, but now what she was doing had a forbidden sense about it as she impaled herself on a black man and immediate she shuddered in orgasm and cried out in pleasure as the powerful waves of pleasure swept over her.

Ted began to thrust into this beautiful white woman. Even though her husband was well hung her vagina was wet and tight and the beautifully little blond bitch was coming just from being fully penetrated by him and now as he thrust into her she was having even stronger orgasms.

Anne kept herself fit and by tightening her muscles just right she could force her husband to come in her – right now she wanted this black man's sperm in her and she began to practice her art all the time reveling in orgasms.

Ted could feel what she was doing to his cock and he was delighted. Soon he could no longer resist and he began to pump his sperm into this sexy little bitch. He wished he could impregnate her but he realized that day was probably long gone.

Dan was taping everything and was delighted with his anniversary gift.

Anne was delighted that she followed her instincts and fucked this wonderful black stud. The question now in her mind was how many times could she fuck him before she had to give him up.

They fucked three more times and felt like more. Dan was out of tape so he left Anne and Ted alone while he went out of the hotel to purchase more. The time allowed Ted and Anne to be alone and fuck again – this stud was insatiable and so was she. Now they could tell each other how they felt about each other – each wanted the other as often as possible.

Dan returned and continued to videotape until in an interlude, Anne asked him to stop. She said he had received enough of his anniversary gift, but she had not.

"Dan, she said, "I'm having a wonderful time with Ted and … Well; I want to spend the rest of the night with him. I want to be alone with him."

Dan smiled and then kissed her and said, "I'll just watch my beautiful bride enjoy her anniversary present." He sat down in a wing chair which offered the best view, as Anne asked her black stud to fuck her again.

Desiree Davidson

The Three of Us

The girl who answered the door was a living doll. She had long brown hair swept back by a green hair band. Her eyes were a light grey. Her face was beautiful and what a figure, revealed in a white eyelet blouse tied at midriff and a pair of emerald green short shorts revealing great legs and the soft contours of an inviting cunt. She was braless and her large hard nipples were jutting out through the fabric. She had an ivory complexion which was repeated in her arms and long legs. She was about 5 feet 5 inches and all of her was hot. In short, she was drop-dead gorgeous!

"Hello," I said, "I'm Eric."

"I'm Janet," she said as she invited me in.

"James will be back in about 20 minutes-he had to run to the store," she said.

"I hope you'll like the meal I've made tonight it's a simple homemade Chinese dinner,"

Janet said, "Come sit at the kitchen table."

"James said you're from Oklahoma."

"We're both from the same town in Tennessee," she said.

I sat down at the table and positioned myself so the bulge in my pants wasn't so obvious. I had gone rock hard the minute I saw her. I wondered how I could have this sweet little doll. As I was thinking of how I might seduce her, she was telling me about the town where they both grew up and said they were high school sweet hearts. James was 22 and she was 21.

I loved to look at her and she loved to show off her beautiful body. She came over to the table and leaning over to set the places the three unbuttoned buttons of her blouse gave me a beautiful view of her 34–C breasts; almost exposing her nipples, which I noted were hard.

I was thinking about how nice it would be to fondle and kiss and suck her lovely breasts and nipples. Just then I heard the apartment door and James came in with a jar of Chinese mustard.

"Hi Eric, I'm glad you could make it through the snow. At least it's Friday and we won't have to get out tomorrow to go to Weapons Systems Control School", he said.

I noticed his words implied I would be spending the night.

"I'd love to spend the night with his wife and him, and do a lot more than sleep!" I thought.

Soon Janet had everything ready and we sat down to a delicious meal. As we ate they asked me to tell them of my life in Oklahoma and how I ended up in the Navy. They then reciprocated and told me about their life in Tennessee.

Toward the end of the meal, I said, "James, you didn't tell me you had a great cook and a drop-dead gorgeous wife!"

Janet said, "I'm glad you liked it and me."

That made me do a double take for I suspected I was about to experience a reverse pickup.

James and Janet cleaned up the table and kitchen, and I watched as they moved back and forth. They were well matched. James was about six feet and had a head of curly black hair. He was toned but not overly muscled. The outline of his body in his clothes showed a well proportioned man with weight to height just right. Anyone would call him extremely handsome and well matched with his sexy bride.

Things were completed in the kitchen and James said, "Let's go in the living room."

James and Janet sat down on the couch, so James and I were seated on either side of her. We talked some more and got to know each other. I was at one point absent mindedly thinking how much I'd like to fuck Janet when my hand brushed her left breast as I was talking with my hands.

I said "Oh, I'm sorry."

Janet replied, "Don't be sorry, I'm proud of them and looks like you liked the experience." As she said this, she reached over with one finger and lightly outlined my hard cock bulging down my right pant leg.

"I'm highly complimented," she said.

She took her finger away and I swear if my cock wasn't harder and longer than it had ever been.

James said, "Janet went to Chicago this week and bought a few things; she hasn't modeled them for me yet. Would you like to see a brief fashion show?"

Desiree Davidson

Before I could reply, Janet said, "Yes Eric I want to do it for you. You can tell me if they are sexy enough."

Janet got up and went in the bedroom.

I wondered what could be sexier than the outfit she was wearing at dinner! I was about to find out: She came out in a red bikini which was just great with her brown hair. The top was not padded and her beautiful breast filled the cups perfectly and her large erect nipples were plainly outlined through the unlined top. Janet turned for us and struck several provocative model type poses.

Then she went back to the bedroom and shortly returned in a sheer light green baby doll pajama. She was wearing next to nothing and I could practically see all of her beautiful charms. She went through the same modeling routine and then came back a third time.

This time, Janet was wearing a cream colored cross between a baby doll bottom in its sheerness and a bikini bottom. There were little green ribbons at each side to release the panty. The top was even better. It was a little jacket with three green ribbons arrayed down the front. She looked fantastic as she modeled the outfit for us. I noticed as she showed the last outfit to us she released the top two ribbons. James and I both told her we liked the outfit she had on, best of the three. Janet instead of returning to the bedroom came back to the couch and sat down between us.

As she sat down she said, "I want to really see what effect I have on you two sailors."

I was hard and wanted her and I think the couple intended for me to have her, but I wasn't sure how to proceed. I decided to let them take the lead.

We returned to talking about everything of the life of a sailor and his wife. I could hardly keep my eyes off Janet's breasts.

Suddenly, James reached over and un-tied the last ribbon and pulled the sides away so her firm breasts were totally exposed. Then he said, "If you want them, take them. In fact you can fuck her if you want."

"Did I ever!" I thought.

I asked Janet if I could kiss her while I fondled her breasts and was answered by her pulling me toward her for a deep French kiss. The whole time I was fondling her breasts and kissing her, her small hand

was stroking my cock through my pants. I moved down and began to suck her nipples as she continued to stroke my cock.

After about five minutes, Janet said, "Let's get you sailors out of your clothes so I can return the favor.

When I stood up, James was already naked and presenting a 7-inch average thickness dick.

Janet took the filmy little top off and tossed it to her husband but still had on the filmy bottom with the little green ribbons on each side. I finished removing all but my shorts. When I removed them and stood up my hard cock stood proudly against my belly and was seeping pre-cum.

"Janet said, Oh god! James, look at the size of his cock. You two set on the couch for a minute, I want to suck you both--that is if I can get my mouth around the girl's delight he's packing."

James and I sat down on the couch and Janet kneeled in front of us. As she was getting down, James reached over and took my cock in his hand and stroked it and gauged its thickness.

"Janet is going to love this--so would I," James said.

Janet had not eaten any dessert at dinner and she joked, "Now, It looks like I get double helpings of whipped cream."

Janet started on her husband and in a short time made him come. She kept his cum in her mouth and came to me and kissed me so we could share his cum.

When she pulled away from my mouth she said, "My husband usually comes pretty fast. I can suck and fuck all night with a man equipped like you."

As she said it, she was cupping my big balls and commenting, "I bet these guys can keep on going. You are very well equipped!"

Janet began to suck me and was struggling to take me in, so I suggested we play another game. I stood up and then helped her to her feet. I said I was ready to fuck her now.

James got up and walked over with his dick limp and although his dick was slightly above average length erect, his balls were much smaller than average. I had noted in my mind the quantity of cum was small as she shared his cum with me in our deep kiss.

He stood behind Janet and pulled the ribbons and took the bottom garment away. He said, "Eric you can have my wife. I'd like to watch,

if it's OK with you. Do anything you want with her short of anal or pain."

I picked Janet up and carried her to the bed. I was not surprised it was turned down for this moment. James followed us in and sat down on a chair. I lay Janet down on the bed and moved between her legs to fuck her face to face. She reached for my cock to position it in her wet pussy. I told her to stop and I asked her husband to take my cock and position it--thus he officially gave me his wife!

She was very wet and ready. I entered her gently. I moved with very gentle motion allowing her to adjust to my cock. When I was fully in, I paused and leaned down and kissed her and asked if she was ready for a good long fuck.

"I'm always ready to fuck as many men as I can get" she said.

"That was an interesting comment," I thought.

Maybe this pretty baby was a nymphomaniac, or hopefully just a normal woman who could never get enough sex. I began to fuck her and I could feel she had a large clit which was being rubbed with my every thrust. About five minutes after I started fucking her, she had her first vaginal orgasm and then just kept on coming for the next fifteen minutes, when I began to shoot long jets of cum into her pretty little body. She felt so good and her beautiful routine of setting this up had me super excited and I shot about seven streams into her cunt. I knew what James wanted from his behavior. I told him to come to his wife and lick the cum out of her cunt. While he was doing that, I told him when he was through, he was to clean my cock of his wife's delicious juices and then suck my cock back up to maximum firmness so I could fuck Janet again.

As James sucked my cock hard again, his techniques made it obvious that mine wasn't the first cock he had sucked. He was definitely bisexual. While he sucked my cock, Janet and I were deep kissing and I was playing with her beautiful breasts. She was a great kisser and I suspected very oral when the cock wasn't quite so large. I held her away from me and I asked if she would like me to cum in her husband's mouth.

She said, "He'll love it, I've seen him take several guys in turn at a party, but what I'd really like, is to watch you fuck his virgin ass!"

James continued to suck and in my mind I speeded up my excitement and began to shoot stream after stream of cum into his mouth. He was in heaven having gotten two loads of cum, one from his wife's pussy and one directly from me while sucking off the man who had fucked her.

We took a break and mostly Janet and I talked as we drank our cokes. It seemed James and Janet held sex parties very frequently with usually 10 to 12 men who had been selected by James from the naval base personnel or occasionally one or two Marines from the group that was stationed at the Ninth Naval District for security and entrance guard detail. They had been doing it for almost a year.

James went to the bathroom and we were alone. Janet told me her husband wanted to try anal sex. He took her that way and she thoroughly enjoyed it. I asked if she would like to have me anally fuck both of them. She said yes, but James had never allowed another man to take her ass, although he did it regularly. She told me the reason he still had a virgin ass was he had not yet felt comfortable enough with any one of my men. I think he is comfortable with you.

I told her I would love to be the first man to take her husband and I wanted her to participate when the time came. She told me she would. James returned in a few minutes and it was a few minutes more before we returned to the bedroom.

Janet told her husband to suck my semi-hard cock to get it fully hard and ready. He went at the task with a passion.

While he was sucking me off, Janet said, "Eric would like to be the first to take your virgin ass. She went on and told him if he was satisfied with the experience she would like to give her ass to me as well"

James said, "I would like to try you and you can have my wife anytime, but no one else but you and me."

When he had me fully hard, I told James to lie on his side so I could lubricate his anus with the Vaseline Janet brought to me. I stretched him with lubricated fingers until three fingers entered easily. He was relaxed and ready. I had Janet lubricate the head of my cock and the entire shaft. Her talented hands stroked my cock and it felt wonderful. When lubrication was completed, I asked James to lie on his back with his legs open. As he took the position, I noted his dick

was only semi-hard. I lifted his legs over my shoulders and asked Janet to take my cock and guide me as I entered him, and in this way symbolically give me her husband to fuck.

She held my cock and I gently entered head deep. Then I allowed him to relax, and I eased past his sphincter muscle and gently pushed in the full length of my cock. I asked if he was ready. He said yes and I told Janet to lay her head on his stomach and take his dick in her mouth and suck him off while I fucked him. I began to take long slow strokes and just as he cried out he was coming. I went to rapid thrusts and raised my excitement level so my cock began to shoot cum into his ass. James was no longer a virgin. He was a confirmed bisexual. I pulled out of him and went to the bathroom to cleanup. When I returned, James headed for the bathroom.

While James went to the bathroom, Janet and I made out kissing and fondling. I asked her if she was ready to have another man's cock in her ass. I would love it, but let's ask James if he is sure, again. When James returned I asked him if he would give me his beautiful wife's ass. He eagerly said he wanted me to be her second in and asked if he could be involved. I told him he would do the same thing to give his wife to me as she had done, and after he had guided me in, he could fondle her breasts and kiss her while I fucked her.

I pulled Janet's beautiful legs over my shoulders and James took my cock and guided it as I entered her. Janet had never been stretched this much so I went very slowly. When she was relaxed I began long swift thrusts and rocked her world. She started coming just like she did when I was in her cunt--she was truly a hot little number--orgasmic in every department. She was wonderful. She literally milked cum out of my body with her anal muscles. What a sexy doll!

When I finished, I went to the bathroom to clean up. When I came back it was almost as if they didn't expect me to come back so soon, for they were talking in hushed tones.

They looked up and Janet said, "Would you spend the night with us and stay with us through Saturday too?"

I told them yes, I would love to be with them. Where will I sleep?" I asked.

Janet said, "You will sleep with me and if you want my husband you can take him in the living room on the thick, soft rug."

James said, "We want you to take us separately or together in any way you choose."

Janet went to the bathroom to clean up and gave me the chance to make fully sure James was alright with what Janet said and he was in full agreement.

When Janet came back, I proposed we have one more together session before I took her to a single man bed.

I said, "I want James and me to do a double penetration of your pussy."

Janet was concerned about my cock size but was ready to try. I had James lay on the bed on his back. I sucked his dick a few minutes to get him totally hard and then I had Janet impale herself on him with her face looking at his feet. I then eased her back so she was totally lying with her back on her husband's chest. James's dick was firmly in her about four inches. I had them spread their legs and I kneeled over the couple and placed my cock against James's dick and slowly opened up Janet's cunt. I felt the head of my cock move over the head of James's dick and I thrust in several more inches. I had James make short rapid thrusts in his wife while I took longer thrusts.

My cock was pressed against her clit with every thrust and very soon the pretty baby was coming on us. In only a short time, James began to shoot his cum. I felt the warmness of his cum coat my cock. His dick softened fairly rapidly and he pulled out leaving his wife for me to finish as he held her. I fucked the beautiful bitch for several more minutes and then proceed to fill her cunt with cum.

We separated and the three of us lay on our sides together. James was behind Janet and Janet and I were facing.

I asked, "Are you sure you want to have sex in separate rooms?"

They both agreed it was what they wanted. I asked James to move off the bed. Then I placed Janet on her back. My cock was hard again and I had James once again give me his wife by placing and guiding my cock into her pussy. As we fucked I heard the bedroom door open and close and we were truly alone. When I finished in her, I had her kneel over my face so I could lick my cum out of her cunt and stimulate her clit with my tongue to bring her to some mind blowing chain orgasms.

Desiree Davidson

It was already early morning and I had been cuddling Janet in my arms for a couple of hours.

She got up to use the bathroom and when she returned she said she wanted to sleep for awhile. When she was asleep, I left the bedroom and went to the living room and found James awake and waiting.

I prepped him with lubricant and had James stand by the sofa and lean over the arm. I was already hard having cuddled Janet's sexy little body. I placed my cock against a well lubricated ass and shoved my cock into James. After a few minutes of thrusting his dick shot cum into the side of their sofa, as my large cock had massaged his prostate to orgasm. I fucked him for about 15 minutes and then I blasted off in him. He really felt good and if I closed my eyes I could imagine my cock's next turn at Janet.

James and I went to the bathroom and I made him clean me up. I left and he finished up himself. When he returned I had a ready cock for him to suck. He obviously had lots of practice for he was adept at orally pleasuring a man.

I went back to the bedroom and found Janet on her side. As I cuddled her my hardening cock was pressed into her legs just below her cunt. As she slept, I pulled her legs up to gain entry as we spooned. I fucked her gently for a long time. The gorgeous bitch had orgasms in her sleep and did not wake. As I was also growing sleepy, I stepped up the pace and filled her cunt with cum.

The next morning, my hosts were rejuvenated and ready for more sexual play and it continued well into Saturday night.

On Saturday afternoon, they got out their photo album and showed me photos of their parties which always lasted from 8 o'clock Friday evening until 2 o'clock Saturday afternoon about once a month. The photos confirmed Janet took between 10 and 12 men at each of their parties. I was an invited guest at their next party and quite the star!

en you walked in and stripped off your clothes, as you asked if I had a good time.

"I wanted to shout to the world I had his big cock and I had orgasms before, but these were orgasms! He took me like I had never been taken," I thought. There was no way to answer your question fully, so I said softly, "Yes!"

You slipped in to our bed beside me and kissed me and told me you loved me and you'd like details. Eric you asked me to kneel above your head so you could lick my lover's cum from my thoroughly dilated vagina and I told you all Stan and I did, from the classroom to the final. We finished in more ways than one and were lying together facing.

You were prepared for my question, Stan and you had talked as he left and the two of you had already agreed if I wanted it.

"Eric," I said, "I want to be with my Stan again--alone--as soon as possible."

You said, "He'll pick you up here Friday after school and take you to his home for the weekend, and his girl friend Susan or 'Wild Thing' as I came to christen her, would spend the weekend with me, Eric.

We agreed this was what we wanted, and the swap is what happened, for that first weekend and a significant number after.

There were many times we had that threesome we had initially planned, but as the months progressed, you told me you enjoyed watching us two as much as you enjoyed doubling me. You told me I was so beautiful and totally responsive with him. You said you had never seen anyone have the intensity of orgasms with him that I had with him. He seemed to know exactly what I needed and could deliver it. You told me that we were the most perfectly sexually matched couple you had ever seen.

Christmas came and you planned a surprise for me. I bought you an electric train that year, because I kept 'remembering' my child-hood train. You had bought me a sexy lingerie outfit and matching high-high heels. It was pale mist blue. It consisted of a little string ribbon tie sheer jacket falling just below my breasts, the French cut panties were also ribbon tie at the sides, the garter belt and hose were a perfect match to the bra and bikini. I asked you to open your gift first, and you told me it was just what you'd had when you were a boy. Then I opened mine.

Desiree Davidson

You asked me to go to our bedroom and put it on and then let you see me by the Christmas tree.

You said Stan had been waiting in our dark kitchen and quickly came out, stark naked with a huge erection from just from hearing my pretty voice and the anticipation of having all of you. You quickly tied six ribbons at two inch intervals, each with a bell on his erect cock. He stood just in the darkness of the kitchen off the dining room where we had the Christmas tree. I came back to the tree and you told me I was a vision of sexual excitement.

You said that you had another gift and came to me and kissed me until Stan could be standing behind me.

We finished the kiss, you quickly moved aside as I opened my eyes and saw Stan.

You said "I'm giving you your lover for Christmas.'"

He stepped to me and took me in his arms and I kissed him and I touched the bells and ribbons and asked, "What are these for? Do they have a purpose?"

You said they do and Stan kissed me as he slipped the ribbons loose on the jacket and took the jacket off exposing my beautiful breasts to his hands and mouth.

You untied the ribbons at the panties sides and my lover, and your fellow 'Hunter' picked me up in your stockings and high heels and carried you to our bed and lay you down.

You told me that you had never seen any woman lubricate and relax so fast, as Stan positioned above me, I placed him for entry and he slid in two inches. You removed a belled ribbon, he went four; we proceeded as you told me at each bell ring, his next 2 inches was another gift from you. When you removed the sixth, you told me how much you loved me, and you said you wanted only the best sexual partner for me. I was with him many times before, but as Stan fully penetrated me with 14 thick inches, you said that we were so beautiful together and I came solely on the gentle slow penetration and your words. You kissed me, told me he was all mine, and I was all his, and to enjoy myself. You said you would be sleeping in the bedroom across the way. I wrapped my stocking covered legs around Stan's back and held him as to receive his last streams of come. You told me that seeing my pretty heels on his back was so erotic.

Desiree Davidson

As we made love, you watched us through the open doors, and you set up your train. You said that seeing the two of us and hearing the sounds of sex and the beautiful sounds of the two of us coming was fantastic.

We had threesomes, but as a couple Stan and I had the greatest joy in sex. Our relationship continued into the fall, when you accepted a job with Mobil in Dallas. While you were away, Stan came to our home many times, and we never stopped until the moving van pulled away when school ended for me.

Desiree Davidson

Coed Season

Donna you told me to sit on the couch in front of the fireplace and we would eat there. Since it was August, the AC was on and perhaps a little too cool. I got up and walked to the breakfast bar and watched you making sandwiches at the cabinet. As I watched, I noticed you really had a great body--beautiful legs, very curved and as you moved and caught the cold air of the air conditioning across your blouse, your nipples grew hard and it became obvious you were braless. I admired your beauty as you worked, and then remembering the AC was a little cold, I asked if I could turn it up. You told me the thermostat was just down the hall just before yours and Rick's room. As I turned it down, I looked into your room and noted the king size bed was deeply turned down and ready for use.

I came back into the den and you were on the couch and the sandwiches and our drinks were on the coffee table. As I sat down beside you, I thought of all my wife's friends who I had seduced in the few years we'd been married, and I thought, what would be wrong with one more, for I've already done the harm? Our marriage had not cured my sex addiction or hunting as I had hoped.

We ate and talked and flirted. Suddenly, you lifted your pretty bare legs over mine. I stroked them and your bare mid-riff, as both of us continued to flirt--then wanting more, I lifted you up (how small you were) and pulled you on to my lap to kiss you, fondle your breasts, and introduce you to my hardness.

I commented on no bra, and you teasingly asked me how I knew you had anything on. It hit me I'd seen no panty lines in the tight fitting short shorts when I had checked out your firm cheeks as I'd followed you to your car to open the door for you. I paused, thinking for a moment. Perhaps you thought I was not committing fast enough. You suggested to me I was welcome to find out for sure. Without hesitation, I picked you up in my arms as we laughed, and I carried you to your bedroom and lay you gently on your bed.

First I took your blouse off and exposed your beautiful firm breasts. Your nipples were hard (not from air conditioning but from excitement). They and their areolas were dark pink and quite large for a

little girl. Remember how I spent a long time caressing your breasts and kissing you. Perhaps too long, for in a little while you reminded me that I'd brought you in there to determine something. Without hesitation, I unbuttoned and unzipped your shorts and carefully pulled them down over your hips and cleared the zipper over your Mound of Venus, for you were truly naked. I then removed them from your legs, leaving you so pretty.

Sensing you wanted to move right along; I quickly shed my clothing and stood beside the bed, and asked if we needed to do anything. I always asked and complied, but to me, if there is no skin contact, and fluid exchange, then there is no real sex.

You said, "No silly, I want to feel you come in me. You are even better than I imagined!"

With that, I grew even more excited in anticipation of filling you, my cuddly little girl. I remember I started to move between your legs and you had me stop and take the other pillow and place it beneath your round firm cheeks. You said you liked it that way, to get maximum penetration. I think this time, you got more penetration than you expected or had ever had before. I think every time we played, we made love three, four, or five times, then cleaned up together in the shower, and sometimes played again in there, and then we headed back to campus. You beautiful little girl--you were a lot of fun!

One day, late in the semester, as we loved each other, I said you were developing a little bulge in your board-flat, stomach and that your uterus was softer when I deeply penetrated you and accidentally touched it, and your nipples and areola were enlarging and taking on a darker color. I was moving in you as I said it and we were both rapidly approaching orgasm. Hearing me say that, Donna you came so hard! Then you returned to reality just as I began mine.

You said, "Eric you've made me a mother!"

Talk about men not liking to commit! I pulled out of you as I was coming. I streamed across your once flat-belly, and across your changing breasts and left a lot of white creamy pearls in your brown hair. One stream even hit you in the left eye, occluding it for a time, one of your grey blue eyes I was always so fond of looking into when we made love!

Desiree Davidson

Still kneeling over you, my normal brain returned to half functioning, and I said, "How?"

I was still fully erect as always, and I maintained, only with the stimulation of looking at you. I was slowly streaming, for I had not finished. You leaned up, reached out and took hold and stroked the last creamy cum out of me, directed it to pool in your little dark brown fluff of hair, You asked what I thought my package and creamy liquid was for?

I laughed and then I collapsed beside you, stroking you gently, holding you like I'd never done before, as you explained that Rick could not father a child due to a childhood illness, and would cooperate in no other way, so you had elected me to be the father of your child-- and had a great time doing it and wanted me now so much more!"

Desiree Davidson

Come With Me

It was a nice restaurant in the old part of Austin, Texas which at the time had become quite chic.

The couple had been seated just after I was seated. I had already noticed her in the waiting area. She was a beautiful blonde, slim with a firm beautiful ass and full C-cups. She was wearing a short yellow dress with spaghetti straps--almost a sun dress--the weather was unseasonably warm. She had on light green high heels and no stockings were visible. She looked to be about 28. She had a pretty tan. He was dressed in casual clothes, slacks and a polo shirt and brown loafers. By chance, they were seated at a table angled just so I could see them both. I guessed they were married to each other from their rings and how they responded to each other. There appeared to be an element of hostility between them.

I was dressed much like the man except my shirt was blue instead of green. I was out looking for a meal, but I was also looking for a filling dessert of a beautiful woman to make love to.

The thought came to mind I had never tried getting a woman to follow me away from her husband. The more I thought about it, the more I liked the risk and I selected it as my sexual adventure for the evening.

The rib eye steak I ordered and the 'fixings' were delivered in short order. The couple I was interested in was having salad and smaller cut steaks. I hurried through my meal and ordered coffee and paid the bill. I watched the couple the whole time I ate classifying them for a proper approach in this new adventure. Of the pair the woman was dominate. In my mind I was already making her mine.

The couple was within five minutes of finishing their meal when I went over to the beautiful blonde and whispered in her ear, "Leave him for tonight--teach him a lesson for what he's done, you're too beautiful for him, come with me and I will give you a sexual experience you'll never forget. Now get up and tell him you're going with me and I'll bring you home in four hours; you will be perfectly safe."

Desiree Davidson

The blonde got up and whispered to him exactly what I had told her and then she walked out hand-in-hand with me. Her husband never moved and sat there stunned.

I put her in my car and drove to my hotel. She was laughing in the excitement of actually doing what I told her and it working. I was pretty pleased too, I had her.

I'm Janelle," she said, "I never dreamed I would go with a man who asked me on the spur of the moment."

As we parked I asked her if she was sure she wanted to have sex with me. She confirmed she was. I leaned over and kissed her gently and then we kissed with more passion.

"Let's go," she said.

I opened my door and went around the car and opened Janelle's door and caught a glimpse of her beautiful legs. I took her hand and led her to my room.

My hotel had turn down service so the bed had already been turned down. The room was large enough to have a small love seat and one wing back chair. I directed her to the love seat and we began kissing and I fondled her breasts through the sheer fabric of her dress. Her nipples were large and easily excited. The feel of her lightly tanned satin smooth legs was wonderful.

I walked to the bed and took the two chocolates the maid had left on the pillow and returned to the love seat. I gave her a chocolate from my pillow and asked her if she would show me her charms for a chocolate.

"Give me both of them," she teased, "and I will give you me!"

We struck a deal as I handed over the second chocolate.

Janelle stood up and un-zipped her dress and let it fall to the floor. She stood before me with bare breasts, panties and high heels.

I said, "You can take the panties off but I want you to keep your pretty high heels on."

In the soft lamp light I could see that although her mons was closely cropped, my pretty baby was a natural blonde.

She came to me and I took her in my arms and kissed her several times. For the third time I asked her if she was sure she wanted to make love with me.

"Yes, I want you," she replied.

Desiree Davidson

I placed her on the bed. She watched as I removed my clothes. When I was fully naked I could no longer conceal my big cock. It was throbbing against my flat belly and ready to have this lovely dessert. Janelle took me in her hand as I stood by the bed and then she invited me to fuck her. I moved between her legs and with one finger, then two, then three in her wet cunt. I determined she was ready and relaxed. She took my cock in her hand and guided me into her cunt. What a marvelous cunt she had, she tightened her muscles and it was obvious she knew her technique well. I moved completely into her and allowed her to get accustomed to my size and then we began a twenty minute fuck. Janelle was highly orgasmic and she came for several minutes as she cried out, "Oh God! You feel so good…that's it keep fucking me harder!"

Eventually I could not resist having my dessert and as I cried out in ecstasy I shot streams of creamy cum into her. When we finished, I immediately moved into a 69 position so she could lick my cock and I could lick my cum out of her pussy and tongue her pink clit. This brought us to beautiful simultaneous orgasms. Then we lay in each other's arms.

We lay resting for a time but continued to touch faces, lips, breasts and cock and cunt as we enjoyed just being with each other. Janelle told me her favorite position was woman astride and she would like to do that with me. I said that would be wonderful. Then I noted the time and realized we had been having our private party for three hours since we left the restaurant. I asked Janelle how long it would take to get to her place--she said they lived out by the lake; so it would take an hour to get there. I told her to call her husband and tell him she was having such a great time she had decided to spend the night. I laughed as the horny little nymph came back into my arms. I asked her what he said--all he said was I'll expect you in the morning.

Janelle, my special sexual adventure, continued into the early morning. Eventually she slept. I held her as she went to sleep. I did not sleep, for when I feel like I felt that night I never need sleep and I never get tired and with a continual adrenal rush my body goes sexually for days. In the early sunrise, she stirred awake and she called me back into her body for another session of beautiful sex. Janelle was a living doll

who liked everything I liked. I did take her home and her husband was already gone for the day, so we made love one last time in her own bed.

Desiree Davidson

A Black and White Fever

Ann, you were a delight, every time I saw you--at the grocery store picking up a few things on the way home, at events at the elementary school where both our children went, and around the stores in the village square. My Bride knew you, and if we were together, and you waved your little flirtatious wave, then she thought nothing of it. Sometimes we would meet and talk, so it wasn't like we didn't know each other--after all we lived in the same pine forest north of Houston. You were a flirt, a scamp, a tease--and you were in my forest and very quickly became this hunter's deer--and with all that, you were intelligent, well spoken, dedicated to the school, your church, and gorgeous!

Eric, I agree I was a scamp, but it was your fault I was a flirt and a tease, for I only was when you got near me; it wasn't that I just wanted to 'jump you,' but I was awfully curious about a man who's wife never at any time said anything bad about him, and, in fact praised you! You were just too good to be true--and that made you terribly attractive to me.

Ann, I remember one Saturday, I was in the Village Square running errands for Desiree, and you were there as well, and both of us were childless--what were the odds of that with my three boys and your three girls. We nearly matched in age and having our children later, they were of similar age. It was already a Houston summer even though we'd hardly left spring. You had your long brown hair in a pony tail and pulled back through a light emerald green ball cap, tight, light emerald green shorts (cut a bit high on leg and cheek--I wondered if you'd altered them for effect, for I knew you sewed), cute, white, seductive sandals, and a thin low cut, collarless, white blouse and nothing else, and as we talked, you unbuttoned a few more buttons (tease!) on your blouse.

I suggested that we go in the '50's-Look-Ice Cream Parlor' and have something to cool off, and you led me in to the most isolated booth in the back. I intended to hunt you and you had already given

clear indication you weren't going to run away on first approach, so we were actually well along in the clearing of constraints. We ordered and the place was almost empty after we were served.

Eric, when we met, I thought what luck! I would have followed you anywhere that day, and I even made a thinly veiled suggestion when we had been alone with our drinks for awhile. You acted like you didn't even hear it and moved on. I was a bit miffed, I had been rejected, although gently. My emerald green eyes became quite moist, and you reached over the table to me and used your handkerchief to dry the few tears. You told me it takes time, everything is better with time. I knew there would be no seduction this day. There was much of you learning about me, cautioning me about some of the feelings I had expressed earlier, and always that horrible phrase of yours--'Ann, you have to be sure!' You warned me several times about being sure. In the end I was sure--I was the elect--but not fulfilled. You said, at the right time we will meet in the 'forest.'

Eric, I can't claim purity before marriage, or fidelity with my husband--he was gone a lot as an international airline pilot. I had needs, but three girls and my visibility in the community made it difficult to fulfill them all when Brad was away for so long. A 'forest' you told me, and I remembered the time on the jogging trail, when I had led a hunk of a man into the forest and gave myself to him. There would never be a bed of pine needles again--unless the guy was irresistible, like you!

Ann, we met several other times. You lived on the third cul-de-sac over from mine, and I would occasionally jog that way. One day I jogged your way and decided to ring your door bell. I had met your husband at a school function, so it would be no big deal if he answered. He did not, you did and the girls were staying at friends for five hours that evening. You were going to a women's auxiliary function at church and you were getting ready in peace. You quickly told me you didn't have to go; you were just one of the officers and you had about four hours before you had to pick the girls up. I only had two hours, and if the times could be combined for six hours, it would not have been enough to cherish you.

Eric, I asked you in, and we had a quick exchange of information and you asked to stay awhile, and I did cancel my plans. I invited you

upstairs to talk to me while I changed to something else--I was thinking quickie--but you were thinking properly cherished for eternity. I gave you cause for the names you've called me. I was dressed up and when I removed my dress, you were very visible in your jogging shorts and were rock hard. I had checked you out every time we'd met and you always gave me the nicest compliment any man could, by responding to my beauty. I wanted to see close up. You got up and walked to me and kissed me very gently to see what I would do, and then started kissing me most passionately. My beautiful body was available to you, but your hands and fingers were on my hair and face, but I had glued myself to your body.

You stepped back and said, "Ann, you have not run, you are committed, and I want to make you mine--but not now--there is not time to properly cherish you so I will always remember you. We could play like teenagers for a while, though!"

I agreed I would like that, and you removed my high heels, my stockings and my lingerie, all the while praising and kissing my body. Then you removed your jogging shoes and clothing, and we stood apart looking at each other. I'd never seen anyone like you.

Eric you turned down the cover of my bed as I watched. Then you picked me up, carried me over and lay me gently down on my bed, and joined me. There was a lot of talk about the two of us, but for the most part it was a fantastic make out session, hotter than I'd ever had when I was young, with the hottest boy I ever had. There was no intercourse and you only let me get you off once, when I told you we were trying to have another baby--hopefully a boy for my husband. You let me stroke and tongue for it was all I could do--it made me realize how small my hands looked on you and how small my mouth was. You on the other hand taught me what you could do with my large firm breasts. You actually looked to see if I had implants--I saw you but I didn't tease you about it. Besides I had nipple sensitivity to the edge of being orgasmic to the right tongue, and yours was it. You went down on me and kept me coming for most of the last hour of our make-out-session. When I was fully dressed, you did lie back on my bed for a 20 minute hand session and at the end you soaked my hand and wrist and spurted far beyond many times, spotting sheets and carpet."

Desiree Davidson

Ann, I hated to leave you, but I had promised Desiree, I'd be there. I told you the time would come for us to meet in the 'beautiful forest' where time seems to stand still. I actually thought my pretty target was going to be a 'new pregnant mommy-to-be' in a short time, and I admit I moved you to next year in my mental to-do-list.

About two months later, after work I stopped to pick up some items from the store. My timing in getting to the store was very regular at that time in my life, for my professional life had entered what turned out to be a very short lull. The little travel and regularity of schedule for my family was good, but the lack of adventure was killing me. You came running to me like you were looking for me and said you needed my help--right now, that you had done something really stupid! I said ok and you led me out to my company car--I think you had spotted it there and that's why you came to me. I put you in and got in myself and you started to talk a mile a minute about what you had done and why you had come for me. What had you done, Ann?

Eric, I had gone off birth control pills to try for a new baby boy. My husband was taking longer and longer flight schedules and he wasn't meeting my needs in fatherhood or lover or rake. He was supposed to be home that day, and I was supposed to pick him up at the airport, but he called me and told me they needed a Pilot out of LaGuardia for a three leg extension. I was so disappointed because he had been away so long, and I was also at my most fertile time. This was supposed to be the night to make a baby boy. Brad went on and said since I was going to come out to pick him up anyway, could I pick up Devon instead. I asked why and he told me he had called his wife from New York, and she had told him in no uncertain terms to not come home--she was through with his womanizing. Brad had been telling me over the several months he'd been flying with Devon as Co-Pilot, that he was the biggest womanizer he'd ever seen, and rumor had it among the flight attendants that he had the equipment for it and knew how to use it."

I went to Houston Intercontinental and picked Devon up. He and his white wife and their young child went to my church--so I knew him on sight. Growing up in Alabama, I'd never even considered a black man before--the locals would have lynched both of us! As we drove back to The Woodlands, he told me to drop him off at the motel,

because he couldn't go home, but he hoped to talk to his wife, Rebecca, and heal their split. He told me he didn't have to fly for 5 days and he would just stay there if they couldn't heal. He presented his story like a wounded little boy, and that was the first mistake in my thinking. I really felt sorry for him, and felt if we talked more about their situation, that I could give him some very good advice on renewing their marriage--after all I was a licensed marriage counselor before my girls came along.

I had actually been walking on the forest trails when the call came and since Brad wasn't coming home, I really didn't feel like dressing up to pick up his Co-Pilot.
I had on a pleated sky blue skirt just like a short tennis skirt that really showed off my legs, matching cotton panties, white walking shoes, sky blue puff-ball socks, and a button-down-the-front, white, cotton, eyelet, sleeveless blouse, and no bra--I didn't need it because I was so naturally firm--'53 Cadillac bumpers' was what my husband lovingly called them, oddly enough '53 was my year of birth.

As I'd walked the trail in the forest, I thought of you, and wondered when you would be back. I was ready now, whenever you met me this time I was prepared. I went nowhere without my diaphragm and spermicidal jelly. I know you are going to laugh, but I thought this would be a good afternoon to see if I could catch you Eric and consummate; my mother had come to be with the girls--I never dreamed how important it might be to be prepared for you, but just in case, before I left to go to the airport, I placed my diaphragm. I had a couple of guys--well four--since our petting session and the diaphragm had worked perfectly."

Eric as we headed north on I-45, I began to talk to Devon about some things to consider as he talked to his wife. I had not gone far when I exited to his motel. He checked in and I drove around back to his room. I had Brad's convertible and Devon just reached over and pulled out his clothes bag. While he opened the room and went in, I got his dolly and flight case out of the trunk and took it in and closed the door behind me. I wanted to talk some more and he agreed that it would be nice. I launched into my best marriage counseling advice and we had a nice conversation. In the conversation he began to slip in compliments--if he hadn't, I would have been offended--he had already

thoroughly checked me out in the car as the wind blew my short skirt and loose deep-cut v blouse. I admit growing up where I did, I'd always heard stories about how savage and well equipped black men were, and here I was sitting on the edge of the bed with one, who was a know womanizer with a penchant for white woman, according to my husband."

Eric, womanizer or not, I admit I unintentionally made the first move. We had talked about 30 minutes and he had his full flight uniform on except the cap. I told Devon I wanted to talk to him some more, but he should really change out of his uniform--my husband always did before he'd let me get down to business. He got up and went in the dressing area of the room where I could not see and changed--I thought--Devon walked out fully nude and sporting a mighty compliment for me. He was beautifully muscled--all over! He asked me if I liked what I saw.

I simply said, "Yes." "I grew up in Alabama, but I've never seen a black man naked."

It was terribly corny, but he said, "I grew up in Houston, but I've never seen YOU naked--don't you think we should even the score!"

He walked over to me and without asking he started to unbutton my blouse. I didn't stop him--it was so forbidden from everything in my childhood upbringing it made this encounter more exciting than anything I'd ever done, except the sexual dance I'd been doing with you, Eric. I touched him and he touched me and before I knew it, we were in a wild but short make out party on the bed. He was not a gentle man and I liked it. He rolled me over on my back, spread my legs and I took him and placed him into my wet vagina. As I encircled his black back with my long white legs, he thrust into me and with his length unseated my diaphragm, and practically pressed against my cervix, pulsed ten long streams of black sperm into me. I wanted up, but he held me there--there was only a small loss of erection--then he grew hard and took several very long hard strokes and came in me again just as strongly as before. He pulled out and asked if I didn't think the second time was always better. I am extremely vaginally orgasmic and with the excitement of the forbidden nature of what I had just done, I had chains of orgasms each time. Now, he was through with me!

Desiree Davidson

I knew I was in trouble, for there wasn't enough spermicidal jelly in my vagina and on my cervix to kill everything this black stud had pumped into me. I got dressed as quickly as possible as he pretended I didn't even exist, and I ran out to my car. I sat down in the car's leather bucket seat and I realized I didn't have my panties--the Bastard had taken them for a souvenir! I could feel back flow from my well dilated vagina--that was good--get him out of me. My husband kept his golf clubs in the trunk, and I got his towel--better a golf towel washed, than pale yellow stains on his white leather seat. I drove toward the Woodlands and swore to call his wife, but I never did. I noted the time as I came near the Village Center and there was what I needed--a white company car--Eric you were in the grocery store.

On the way into The Woodlands, I thought of what I would do if I were pregnant with a black man's baby--I couldn't abort, because I didn't believe in murdering a child--if I had a black man's baby all of my family would disown me, and my husband would put two and two together and divorce me, tear my girls away from me...The scary thing was I might be impregnated as I drove--today was my most fertile day-- the day Brad and I were going to make a baby boy for him."

Suppose, I still had time I thought, what could I do--what might stop it or minimize the probabilities--then I remembered I'd read about studies that showed that women who had multiple partners at the same time rarely get pregnant, but if they do, it is from the superior sperm that wins out--they had said the men's sperm, war with each other to fertilize the egg. I knew of several men I'd been with recently, who would gladly accept the task--but the Warrior I would be honored to give me a baby was I believed, far superior to the black man who had just come in me. I hurried to the Village Square and found you. I led you to your car, and we got in. I told you little, but asked you to drive behind Randall's in the sloped loading dock where we could not be seen. I asked you to come to the passenger's side, I got out, and you got in dropped the seat back flat, unzipped your suit pants and pulled them and your briefs down--there was my Warrior and I climbed on top of you, closed the door and guided you into me and begin to ride as I explained in detail. You wanted summary--how many times and how much? You wanted to be sure you did enough--you ejaculated in me five times in the hour and each time was far more than he had.

Desiree Davidson

Ann, after the fifth you collapsed onto my chest. I told you I did think you would most likely have a baby from this day and the baby would be mine. Now you have to face the fact the baby is mine not your husband's. Your baby will most likely be a boy--I make them about 85% of the time. You've seen my three sons--two of them are much alike, the middle one is not you're probably going to get a match to me or one of the two who look alike. Are you OK with that? If this isn't enough, you may want to seek others right away.

Eric, I was more than OK, and I sought no others and Bradley is yours without a doubt. I still wanted what you had talked of as 'The Forest' and after our baby arrived and the recovery period was up, I came to you again. You were my first (not even my husband), after the arrival of the baby and I showered on your attention in every way to make you know how much I valued my Warrior. At the end of the four hours I could spend with you, you said you still wanted to cherish me.

Ann I had my spies out, your husband was gone for several days, his mother was in for a visit and wanted you to go away so she could have the children to herself, Desiree and the boys went to grandparents for a week, and I took two days off--so I had a messenger bring a letter to your door announcing you had won a 48 hour stay at a famous hotel and spa near the Galleria and that a limo would pick you up in two hours. At the bottom was the instruction to call a number and use the code word "Warrior" if you would be ready. You did, it did and I was in it and we did go to be best hotel in the Galleria and spent two glorious days together. You learned about 'The Hunter' and 'Sex, Honor, and Love, without Constraints' and you never again used the word Warrior in referring to me. I cherished you properly, so I will always remember you.

Eric, 'My Hunter,' I slipped up sometime on those two days or you dislodged my protection this time and I didn't notice--with men like you running around--thank god for birth control pills anyway, Bradley has a brother named Brent and he is yours. You moved away I would have told you. My husband, Brad loves his three daughters, but we might as well say it--he loves his two boys more, and doesn't have a clue he had some help in getting them.

Desiree Davidson

Party

Nick and Jill had never attended a sex party together before and it was something Nick wanted to do more than Jill.

Jill had take thirty-three men as lovers during the first five years of their marriage and perhaps 75 men since she became sexually active at 13, and she wasn't sure she could refuse any man or woman at the party without Nick being disappointed. Besides she didn't like to use condoms and she was sure the men at the party would.

Nick had been with many women before and during their marriage. Indeed, Nick had fucked her best friend Susan, while she had taken Susan's husband in a couple-swap just last week.

Both Nick and Jill liked to watch each other with a new partner and that was what had made her decision final when Nick suggested a sex party, but that was not the main reason.

***

Jill got out of the tub just a few minutes after Nick stepped out of the shower. Jill thought, "My husband's a real stud -- look at the size of his balls and his thick 10-inch long cock. I love the feel of him coming in me. That reminds me; I better put my diaphragm in so I can take some man who wants to fuck me without a condom. She loved the feeling it gave her to feel her lover's semen spray into her body."

Jill was a lucky woman, she did have a wonderful sex partner in her husband, but it was always nice to take a new man on occasion.

Nick had gone into the bedroom. She got out of the foam filled tub and began to dry herself off. As she dried her c-cup breasts, she thought, "I wish my breasts were bigger, Nick was really impressed by Susan's d-cup breasts, and her greedy cunt was very impressed with Nick's big long cock."

Jill dried her cunt and then her long shapely legs. She had great legs, she thought, "Every one of the men she had fucked had told her so. They loved to have her wrap them around their muscled backs and draw their cocks into her wet, tight pussy."

Desiree Davidson

Jill after thoroughly drying herself opened a drawer and took out her case and the spermicidal jelly and placed her diaphragm. She wished she could do without it, but Nick was firm that he wanted to be the father when she decided to become pregnant. She moved and confirmed that it properly covered her cervix – she was ready to fuck any man or men (she was curious about a gang bang – when she was sixteen she had let three football players fuck her repeatedly and it was fantastic – she couldn't believe how many times they had shot their cum into her body before she fucked them dry. She had not expressed this "curiosity" to Nick but it was the main reason she actually agreed to go to a party.

Jill fully nude, walked into the bedroom and caught Nick just about to dress. She walked to him and stroked his quickly stiffening cock and told him she wanted to see his cock buried in lots of delicious cunts tonight – but when they got to the party she wanted him to fuck her first and then let her suck him hard again as she sent him off ready for his next pussy. Nick liked the idea and told her that he would be taking the best pussy first. Nick continued and told her he wanted her to be totally free to do anything she wanted to do – this was her night to enjoy.

Jill asked him, "Anything?"

Nick replied, "Anything."

Nick's fingers found her swollen pussy lips and rapidly developing wetness and almost regretted giving her to other men, but both of them knew their lovers and sex adventures were what had kept their marriage exciting and vital – monogamy would have never worked for either of them.

***

Jill and Nick were greeted by the host and hostess and told that there would be 12 couples at the party but only 3 had arrived and there was going to be three single guests to even up the entertainment of the women. Both Jill and Nick were excited. The host directed them to a bedroom where they could change out of their clothes.

Nick waited for Jill and they walked to the party room and saw the three couples already paired off and fucking away.

Desiree Davidson

There was lots of room on the mats and Nick and Jill took up a spot farthest away from the fucking couples. Jill lay down on her back and Nick moved between her legs and proceeded to kiss her and again tell her that he wanted her to do anything she wanted tonight. Then Jill took his hard cock in her hand and guided her husband's cock into her wet pussy. They fucked for about 10 minutes and then both she and Nick came together as he sprayed his hot sperm into her body.

While they were fucking several people had come in and settled into different combinations. Nick pulled out of her and he moved to lean against a couch and she moved to suck his cock. She was on her hands and knees and proceeded to suck Nicks cock hard. He was almost fully hard when he told her that there was a man behind her who wanted to fuck her. She continued to suck and mumbled OK. She felt fingers open her cum drenched labia and slide into her cunt to make sure she was ready. Next she felt a huge cock head pass her labia and begin to penetrate her – she could take him, but she wanted to see who was about to fuck her and told Nick so.

Jill looked around and saw the Blackest Black man she had ever seen and at that moment felt the biggest dick she had ever had begin to inch its way into her pussy. Nick moved out of the way and Jill and her Black stud moved together so she could rest her upper body on the cushion. Jill would later learn that the Black man fucking her was named Jerome. Right now it was enough for her to cry out excitedly – "God. You wonderful stud! Your dick feels great! Don't ever stop fucking me!" – Just as she began to come on his long thick Black dick.

Jill and Jerome fucked for about 15 minutes and Jill was having wave after wave of orgasms convulse her body as Jerome's dick and balls convulsed and filled her body with the first Black sperm she had ever had.

Jerome pulled out of her and helped her to the mat because her legs were weak and shaking from her orgasms. She lay down on her back with her beautiful long blond hair splayed out over the mat. It was then that she saw her husband watching her and everyone at the party gathered around the watch the Black stud fuck the beautiful sexy blonde. Jerome's semen was gathered in the blond patch of her pussy and left no doubt that she had taken him bare back. The crowd wanted more and so did she and Jerome – he was fully erect again. Jill wanted

to do something. She wanted this amazing Black stud to have all of her.

Jill turned to Nick who was keeling by her. "I want something, she said. I want to let him have all of me."

Nick said, "Do anything you want Baby. What do you want to do?"

Jill said, "I want to take my diaphragm out and let his sperm enter all of me!

Jill really didn't hear what her husband said, but it really didn't matter for she was already taking her diaphragm out and handing it to Nick.

Jerome moved between her legs and his huge dick entered her again. He proceeded to fuck the pretty little blond bitch who wanted his sperm in her womb.

All the men and woman watched them fuck again and called out for Jill to come (which seemed to happen continuously on that beautiful big Black dick) and for Jerome to fill her with his hot sperm.

The crowd stayed and watched Jill get fucked by the Black stud a third time, and then Jerome came in her and pulled out to quickly recover and take another woman who was hungering for his big Black dick.

Jill lay on the mat and caught her breath. Her husband moved between her legs and entered her and almost immediately came in her. By the time Nick was through with Jill, there were several men in line waiting to fuck her. Her gang bank with twelve White men and two other Black men (special guests) proceeded through the night and she could hardly walk when Nick came and told her she had had enough.

At home in a nice hot bubbly tub Jill relaxed and thought of the slut she had been – she wouldn't have changed a thing and certainly not her first Black stud or her gang bang.

Nick came in and laid her diaphragm on the bath edge.

Jill looked at it and wondered what her husband was thinking.

"Jill he said, "I don't want you to ever use this thing again. You can't possibly know how exciting it is to know that another man may be impregnating your wife!"

Desiree Davidson

Jill reached up and touched his face and said, "I think you may have enjoyed the party as much as I did. I'll always be unprotected when anyone fucks me just for you!

Nick said "I invited that Black stud you enjoyed so much to come to our house next Tuesday and fuck you again while I watch."

Jill said, "That's wonderful. Can I fuck him anytime he wants me?

Jill, my baby doll, you can wrap your pretty blonde pussy around that big Black dick anytime you want!

Desiree Davidson

Hot Tub Friends

Teresa and Mark kept their marriage alive and exciting by fulfilling each other's fantasy. It was Mark's turn to name the fantasy and Teresa would carry it out. She was very excited about the latest because she had grown curious about what she would find – there were so many stories and tales she had grown up with. Now at 28 she was going to find out the truth for herself. Mark wanted to watch while she fucked a Black Man!

Mark had done some scouting and found a nice hotel that seemed to be frequented by Black men traveling on business. The hotel had an indoor pool and next to it a small hot tub that would seat four. They checked in and took a walk around the hotel to decide how they would proceed with Teresa picking up a Black stud for Mark's fantasy.

Teresa decided she would wait until about 8 o'clock and see if a suitable man came to the hot tub. If that didn't work she would dress up and choose someone in the hotel bar to approach.

Teresa was a petite brunette and had just bought a skimpy bright red bikini that left nothing to the imagination. The top was unlined and her big nipples stood out proudly. The bottom was a thong and hardly enough to cover her trimmed patch of brown hair. Teresa looked at herself in the mirror and Mark whistled at this first view of her new bikini.

Mark said, "God you are a walking "fuck me sign' in that outfit."

Teresa was pleased. That's exactly what she hoped it would be because she was determined she was going to fulfill Mark's fantasy and her secret curiosity tonight.

They went down to the pool and sure enough there were two good looking muscle Black men in the hot tub. Mark and Teresa joined them and Because of the small size of the hot tub, Teresa was right next to the man the other called Devon. Devon was about 30 and must have worked out because he was ripped.

Teresa hoped the two Black men had just met and were not together, because leaning her leg against his under the bubbling water made a noticeable bulge in his swim trunks.

Desiree Davidson

Teresa was blessed with luck because the other man got up and called back "Maybe I'll see you tomorrow – I've got to go get dressed and take my wife out dancing."

When they had come in, Teresa had laid their towels and belongings on a lounger. She got out of the tub and purposely bent over so Devon would see her exposed ass and barely covered pussy. Then she straightened up and let him see her just right body. The she returned to the hot tub and sat down between her husband and Devon.

Devon said "What are your names. They introduced themselves and Teresa noted that Devon's bulge was significantly larger than it had been before she put on her little show.

Teresa asked if he had brought his wife with him too. He said no and went on and said he was divorced.

Teresa purposely moved closer to him and again stroked her leg across his leg and immediately after that reached through the bubbling water and grasped his swollen dick through the trunks. Immediately she said I'd like to take "this" in my pussy while my husband watches.

Devon looked at Teresa in a long pause and then asked where.

Teresa replied, "In our room."

Devon said to Mark, "Are you OK with this man?"

Mark said, "Both of us want it."

"OK Devon, said, "I'm ready for it.

With that Teresa got out of the tub and led the party in drying off and led Devon to their room with Mark bringing up the rear. Once in the room, Devon took Teresa's bikini off and had her fully naked and then dried her off and then he took his trunks off and freed a magnificent 12 in long, very thick Black cock. Teresa grabbed the towel and dried his muscled buttocks and spent a long time drying his cock and balls. Mark had dried himself and had settled down in a chair to watch the action. He was slowly stroking his own smaller cock as he watched his wife dry that Black monster. He was waiting in excited anticipation of seeing Devon fuck his wife for the first time.

Teresa had just gone off birth control pills and had fucked several men she had desired in the last couple of months without condoms so she was going to give all of herself to this Black man as well. She was actually fantasizing that this Black stud would impregnate her. It built the excitement ever higher and Mark and she had talked about

unprotected sex and he was fine with the idea that another man might impregnate her and it only made his fantasy hotter when he thought a Black man might do it. On questioning him about his fantasy a few days before her learned that possibly being impregnated by a Black man was a big part of it. She just wanted a baby and Mark didn't seem capable of giving her one.

Teresa finished drying Devon and stood up dropping the towel to the floor. Devon bent to kiss her and she received it open mouth. Then he picked her up and carried her to the bed and lay her down well into the king size bed. Then he joined her and sucked her breasts as his long fingers gauged the readiness of her pussy for his big cock. Teresa lubricated rapidly and opened to his fingers. Her cunt was on fire and she wanted to be fucked and told him so.

Devon said, "You sexy slut, you might be ready to fuck a White man but you're not relaxed enough to take my cock."

Teresa insisted that he fuck her now and he moved between her legs. He called Mark over and had him hold his cock while he gently pushed just inside her. When Mark turned loose he was firmly in the opening of her cunt and she was begging that he fuck her; so he gave a hard thrust and penetrated her six inches. Teresa screamed in pain at the same time a wave of orgasms rushed across her body.

"Give me all you got," she cried. He did – bottoming out with the head of his cock pushed snuggly against her tilted cervix.

Devon was letting her relax to his size and she was still having orgasm with him just staying in her.

"This White bitch is so sexy, I could come in her right now," he thought. Then suddenly his balls contracted and he spewed his creamy cum all over her cervix and uterus.

Teresa, felt him cum in her and cried out, "Don't stop fucking me. I've got to have your cock in me."

Her pleading encouraged him to recover quickly and he began to stroke in and out of her pussy wondering how many orgasms this hot little White bitch could have. She was in the throes of pleasure constantly and with her legs wrapped around his back he wasn't going anywhere and certainly did not want to leave this sweet pussy.

About 10 minutes passed and he came in her again filling her body with his hot cum.

Desiree Davidson

Evangelizing Judy

I came in the front door of my house and I heard another woman's voice in addition to my wife's beautiful voice. I walked into the kitchen and Desiree introduced me to Judy--God, she was beautiful--she just oozed sexiness. She had on a white midriff tied blouse and pastel blue shorts and the best set of breasts, ass and legs I'd seen in a long time. Judy lived just down the block two houses. She had a ten year old daughter, Cassie; who wanted to play with James our 2 ½ year old. Cassie had taken James to her house and that allowed Desiree to talk to Judy without interruption.

Desiree was trying to evangelize Judy. Judy never went to church and over the next few months, Desiree convinced Judy to go to church with us. Her husband would not let Kurt or Cassie go with their mother so it was just us. Several weeks of this passed and one Sunday Desiree woke up sick. She was pregnant and her feet were swollen and she was generally miserable. She wanted me to go ahead and take Judy to church.

I drove in her driveway and she walked out to our car. I hopped out and opened the door for her. She looked amazing; she had on a button-down-the-front, light-blue dress that fell just above the knee. She wore high heels with it and a delicate gold chain around her neck. Her blue eyes sparkled. As I helped her in the car I got a generous view of her lovely legs. Somehow seeing them that way was sexier than seeing her in shorts

We went to the early church service and it was a small crowd. Judy had become very comfortable with me over the weeks. We shared a song book and our bodies were touching at the hip. When we sat down to pray she took my hand. It was warm and just touching it made me want to touch all of her. I whispered in her ear that I wanted to make love to her. She did not respond. The last hymn we stood again and this time I took the book away and quietly led her out of church and to my car. She said nothing but she went with me. I drove to a hotel and checked us in. It was 9:50 am. I took Judy's hand and escorted her to the room. When we got behind closed doors I took her in my arms and told her how much I wanted her. She suddenly became a wild cat

and we tore each others' clothes off and soon we were naked with each other.

Judy had creamy skin. My wife had told me that she was 33. She looked more like 23. Her blue eyes sparkled when I suggested we assume a '69' position to get to know each others' bodies. Judy agreed, but first we lay face to face on the pillows and kissed long, slow, romantic kisses and fiery, passionate kisses. Then we assumed our position. She had a delicious cunt covered in golden curls. She knew how to take care of a large man orally and she had me in heaven. Shortly as my tongue ministered to her clit, I took her to heaven. It was a wonderful playtime. When we finished oral explorations I licked my cum off her full breasts and suckled her pretty large pink nipples and then she said she was ready for me. I moved between Judy's long legs and she took my cock in her hand and guided me into her. She was very tight but as I gently entered her, she relaxed to accommodate my size. We fucked like teenagers hurrying to make love before they get caught. Judy was magnificent and the quantity of cum I shot into her body showed her how happy I was to be with her.

I took Judy home and then went home. When I went in both Desiree and James were asleep from their morning play, and I too was sleepy from my morning play with Judy.

Judy and I were together a number of other times and grew very romantic with each other as we made love. Unfortunately after about three months of beautiful love making, I was transferred to Los Angeles. However any time I was in the Dallas area on business, Judy always met me at my hotel and we were new with each other all over again.

Desiree Davidson

The Long Drive Home

Samantha and Gerald were finishing their meal in the 'Sutton County Steak House' in Ozona, Texas as I was finishing mine. I was seated where I could see them all the time and they seemed to be exchanging glances and looking at me and then talking.

They were dressed up. She was wearing an expensive chic green wrap around dress, and sexy spike high heels. He was wearing a western cut suit, had a $3,000 Stetson cowboy hat lying on the chair beside him and had a pair of $5,000 cowboy boots on. They were richly dressed for a Monday night,

I was on my way to visit my technicians in Ft. Stockton after I visited my men here in Ozona. Ozona was a nice little town. The first time I came here one of my Techs told me one man owned almost everything around here. I was about to meet the man.

Gerald got up and came over to my table and asked to set down. He spoke quietly and after introducing himself he asked if I thought he had a beautiful wife in Samantha. I said I thought she was more than beautiful; she is my dream women if I were looking for a sex partner. I had been through this drill a number of times--I was being screened by the husband to share his much younger wife, and I was cutting to the chase.

He made his decision and returned to their table and brought Samantha back with him. She sat across from me.

He introduced his wife and I said, "Samantha I very much want to make love to you."

Samantha said, "I like your looks and want you as a partner, but can you be very discrete and do the kind of things I need done?"

I replied, when I leave your bed there will never be a word said about our love making for the next twenty years and by then it just won't matter." The key thing is I will do what ever you want me to do and I will give you freedom...

Desiree Davidson

Gerald interrupted me and said, "You are perfect for our needs. We live five miles from here will you follow us to our home?"

I followed him down the highway a mile and then turned on to a private road that was better than the best two-lane highway in Texas. When we arrived at the house it was walled and gated. Once inside the mansion courtyard there was a circular drive. Their mansion equaled any grand mansion in Dallas or Houston.

Gerald pulled his silver Mercedes into one of the five garages and the couple came to meet me and we went in together. We didn't stop downstairs; we went straight up stairs to the master bedroom and without ceremony, Samantha and I undressed for play time.

Gerald told me he for the most part liked to watch his wife with new men of her choosing. He said he wanted to just sit and watch me take his wife for the first time.

Samantha was a doll, she was beautiful in body, mind, and spirit as I learned a little about her as we lay on the bed and talked, fondled, and exchanged soft as well as passionate kisses.

Samantha said, "My heart, soul, and spirit are yours tonight. Will you care for me and lead me to the end?"

I thought that was rather cryptic, but I agreed I would do those very things. She had a beautiful 29 year old body and I classed her as a 'Hard Body'--just wonderful to make love to.

Samantha told me she was ready. She wanted face to face and I asked Gerald to come over and place my cock in his wife's cunt. He did it readily and I suspected he was bisexual--we would see. Samantha's cunt was warm, wet and relaxed and my big cock entered her relatively easily. I began to move into Samantha and shortly was giving her maximum stroke length. The pretty baby began to come and as the intensity of orgasms increased I noticed a slight shuddering of her body and a defocused look in her eyes...I had seen this before and I knew I had been selected to be the last.

Samantha cried out in the joy of intense orgasm and I came in her with stream after stream of cum. It was like her pretty body was milking it out of me.

When we finished, Samantha went to the bathroom and I moved over to the wing chair next to Gerald. He was holding a magazine

which had stories of sexual encounters. He called my attention to one story in particular and asked if I had ever done that.

"Yes I have done it several times." I said.

"Is it dangerous," he asked.

I said, "It can be deadly, because there is a sharp line separating pleasure of orgasm from chocking to death."

He said, "After you make love to Samantha a few more times I want you to do it to her. Samantha and I have agreed to ask the man we chose tonight to do it for us."

I said, "I will do it for Samantha--I recognize her need."

Samantha and I did make love several ways orally and when she was ready to make love face to face again, I asked if this was the time she wanted her 'freedom.' She was holding my hand and it tremored and I knew she wanted freedom beyond the captivity of her failing body.

I asked, "Am I correct you have a cancerous brain tumor and it is Stage 5–death in six months?"

"Yes." she said.

She kissed me and said, "I can't face the destruction of my life as the cancer takes me. I want to go now--tonight--and have my 'freedom.'"

"Will it hurt?" Samantha asked.

I held her and I said, "There will be no pain; you will go out in an ecstasy of orgasms, and it is my privilege to help you escape the coming disability and pain of your illness.

I lay beside her and told her I would love her and cry tonight for her leaving this world, but someday I would see her again in eternity.

I said, "Is there any last thing you want to do before we start?"

She kissed her husband goodbye and thanked him for letting her avoid a painful death. He was quietly crying as she came back to the bed. I explained what I would be doing and explained the 'stop signal' to use if she changed her mind--it was simply to touch either of my arms.

She lay on her back and I moved over her and she took my cock and guided me into her. As before, she began to come very quickly and I moved one hand to her throat and then a second and began to stop her

air supply--her orgasms were ten times stronger than the first. She touched my arm and I release the pressure enough for her to whisper.

"Eric, thank you, please do it now!" Samantha said.

I returned to full pressure and without leaving an earthly mark on her beautiful neck, her eyes lost their light and her spirit stepped into eternity. I had come as she died. I moved off of her and pulled her to me and held her as I cried for her. Gerald came over and said, it's all right, she was very ill. Gerald and I placed her back in bed in a sleeping position.

I asked, "What will come of this?"

Gerald said, "Nothing--I own everything around here including the city and county officials. Everyone knows she was terminally ill."

I dressed and he walked me to the door.

He said, "Thank you for giving her so much pleasure in the last few hours of her life."

He shook my hand and I went to my car and the big ornamental gates opened and allowed me to leave.

It is hard to lose a man, but it is harder to lose a woman in this strange life. But now at least Samantha has her 'freedom'. I have always remembered them with joy and rejoiced in being in the right place at the right time to perform this act of service.